past
*im*perfect

Stanley Pelter

To
Kevin
Hope you 'enjoy' 1 or 2
"difficult" ones?
"Read aloud - Slowly"
is my tried & tested advice
Very best wishes
Stanley P

George Mann Publications

Published by
George Mann Publications
Easton, Winchester,
Hampshire SO21 1ES
01962 779944

A CIP catalogue record for this book
is available from the British Library

ISBN 0954629922

also by Stanley Pelter

Coming on Lately

Seventeen is sufficient

i meet U in the inbetweenitee

Pensées

Word Plays

a moment is forever

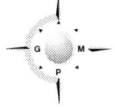

George Mann Publications

to

mum and dad

and to U who gives me belief, space and time,

with love

Contents

Preface

This volume of Haibun, the first of several, is a *Gift Book*. Not an indication of wealth, it is a token gesture away from a culture of overwhelming consumerism. We take it as read that 'money makes the world go round', and that food, clothing, shelter, information, theatre, cinema etc. are gained only after payment to others. All manner of means are employed to increase the amounts we pay. It appears to be a core characteristic of our society and, like many others covering a wide variety of activities, is quickly and often unquestioningly accepted as the prime way communal life can be successfully organised. This is emphasised in a world with a growing population, and where communication can be, in a moment, both local and global. Often those who rail against it do so with fundamentalist fervour. They make a clear statement, going some small, usually horrific, way to effect a reduction in the population. Believed to be able to confront and subdue immense power, it moves lineally, is grossly black and white, hurts too many, is faith based, relies on unproven and unprovable premises, and is often constrictive and repressive.

A small gift may seem a million miles away but, with a few additional factors, there is a commonality of principle and purpose. Those who receive it retain choices. They can reject and bin – in line with that great indicator of organised consumer structures, junk mail; read and pass on to someone else; read and not pass on. If so inclined they can also make a donation to the British Haiku Society[*], a Charity dependent on members subscriptions and financial gift aid.

I suppose that most who read this book will be members of a haiku society or group, and enjoy reading and, perhaps, writing short stories, and so are more likely to empathise with a tiny, ephemeral gesture of opposition. Above all else, the hope remains that, having read some or all of the haibun, it will stimulate and encourage a proactive and creative response.

[*] Send to British Haiku Society Treasurer, Steve Mason, The Basement, 67A Offord Road, London N1 1EA

Introduction

1

Haibun grow on a far-flung patch of the literary garden. With Japanese antecedents, its evolution and development in the West is of recent origin. A haibun fingerprint kit acknowledges that it evolves from, relates to and combines with Haiku, a poetry of brevity and understatement, also of Japanese origin. From this historical base come the qualities and perceived terms of reference and parameters that presently characterize and distinguish it from other formats. At this early stage in its occidental evolutionary cycle, it is, essentially, a short story combined with haiku poetry. Both elements play an equally important part in the completed work. The relationship is complex, replete with unexplored possibilities and more varied than at first may be apparent.

Haibun can vary in prose length from a few to about 8000 words. Examples of the latter are Matsuo Bashô's *Oku-no-hosomichi/The Narrow Road to the Deep North*, David Cobb's *The Spring Journey to the Saxon Shore*, and Ken Jones's *Stallion's Crag*. Although the prose of haibun shares characteristics with haiku, it also differs from it in significant ways. This relationship between these two components of haibun delineates and defines its present structure. Its unique, even peculiar characteristics distinguish it from both mainstream short story and other literary forms. Within the prose language there is recognition of quality and contextual combinations central to the haiku genre but different to others. No self-respecting haibun shows its face in public unless haiku is incorporated as an integral part of the structure. That, until recently, has been an unquestioned, sacrosanct core feature. This hybrid marriage of haiku poetry and connected prose is seen as *the* essential defining link. It is in the application that creativity, expansion, opportunity and additional expression lie. In my view, rather than being a necessity, this is a mind barrier. It is quite possible for a haibun, replete with haiku qualities, to be diminished by haiku. There is a danger that mental barriers are put in place and the permissible is coloured. Although a useful concept to establish specificity, any tightening of borders is an inhibitor. Standards and expectations are defined; formal, contextual, aesthetic possibilities limited. Lateral approaches stay hidden.

Along with the single discipline *short story*, haibun is often perceived as a minor Art form, peripheral to haiku, which is itself distanced from the literary mainstream. The fact that cultural forms are peripheral does not, of course, connote their importance or unimportance. But is haibun one hybrid too far? Certainly, it is not an easy medium to get to grips with but, as with opera and, more importantly for haibun, comic graphic literature, matured in the West by such creators as Will Eisner, Art Spiegelman, Chris Ware, Paul Auster, Alan Moore & Bill Sienkiewicz, Ennis & Dillon, and in the East by at least Tezuka Osamu and Riyoko Ikeda, its impact relies upon the precision of application and creative interweaving of cross disciplines[1]. Presently, manufacturers of haibun utilize and prize the subtleties and specifics of two means of communication. Success indicates a third, and otherwise unobtainable entity is created, one that can challenge the form, layout and content of more traditional genre.

2

The Haiku Society of America has recently defined haiku as being:
   a short poem that uses imagistic language to convey the essence of an experience of nature or the season intuitively linked to the human condition.

Incorporated in this view of what makes haiku are qualities that emerge from an historical Zen perspective. Providing a sensitized backdrop, they should still not form any barrier between their history and the zeitgeist of the Period in which we live. In a recent article I listed some terms of reference and parameters of a prematurely hardening tradition. They include: *haiku and prose integrate, each enhancing the other; the prose component incorporates existing characteristics of haiku including 'lightness', image juxtaposition, season word, 'showing' not 'telling', acute and reinvigorated perception of the seldom noticed and often disconnected, detachment from the author, application of paradox, ambiguity, allusion, an abstaining from abstract and conceptual language, contains a variety of layers and is expressed with musicality; it should be a subtle but in-depth piece of creative work, more effective without two or more haiku set next to each other; a haiku completes it; only small doses of exposition; never is it a 'travel diary'; subject matter is broad but often incorporates autobiographical experiences that relate interior and exterior awareness; there are no emotional or polemical outbursts; it is not just the recording of stimuli.*

3

This first illustrated collection includes haibun that do comply with a number of qualities believed to be the backbone and fibre of haibun. Others are atypical, indicating areas of appropriate development beyond present guidelines. This is not done to be wilful or awkward but rather to delimit parameters, raise questions, extend boundaries and covertly glance at issues that drift about behind the shadows of acceptable consensus. It is not a revolution, more a tentative and exploratory creative dissension. The implications of history, stated and implied developments, are in a different relationship to the norm. & *Y Not?*

Some involve redefining the present tradition of sequential word pattern 'story form' that employs simple and everyday language of logical and lineal sense. In this volume some 'stories' are more cubic, homogeneity evolving from the total image that appears on the page. By definition, because literary effects are minimal and language patterns run counter to familiar formats, there is a need for open-ended reader involvement and understanding. Others use more visual means as accompaniment and participation that highlight one aspect or another of the prose/poetry link. More purposefully, a visual can be a feature of an element to help make an unfamiliar haibun unity, adding a special frisson or resonance otherwise difficult to achieve in other ways. It can either be a 'haiku' in its own right, different and less easy to recognise than those presently thought to be the-end-and-be-all, or it can become that third, 'shock' element in the metamorphic trinity of thesis, antithesis, synthesis; the 'caterpillar', 'pupa', 'butterfly' effect.

A simple example is the short short story 'Venus' where the visual is, at the very least, a 'haiku' equivalent, but also more in that it both reflects the story and juxtaposes with it an image not contained or mentioned in the prose. A visual has an imperative. It is another form of speech, more effectually direct in transformative power, imposing immediacy of meaning. The purpose is to make new connections. It adds a symbolic statement for a close, bright planet seen early morning, unrealistic in everyday terms but logically relevant and, although accurate to the event, in a visual it is more surrealistic and surprising. Words elongate and diminish the spontaneity of this effect. The visually striking vignette of a wartime, alien-looking child, caught in a moment between an intensely felt but inaccurately interpreted experience, the natural acceptance by a child-centred teacher of a learning opportunity, and the warmth of young love (yet another misinterpretation) should, as an additive but integrated part of the prose, be sufficient to achieve the intended effect.

Western haibun is a young genre, still innocent, excitingly open and tempting. There is much to find, explore and incorporate. Walking one path blinds. Edging close, just beyond the cataracts of mist, lay a large number of tributary paths. As evidenced in the Red Moon Press International Anthology of Contemporary Haibun, some, in small groups or alone, have begun their walk. None know where it may lead. There will surely be cul-de-sacs, frustrating returns to starting points, cuts and bruises, losses of direction. But perhaps there will also be a more complex interlinking of consciousness with multi-layered and directional meanings.

[1] There are many similarities between contemporary East and West image stories, but also significant pattern, visual emphasize, structural, subject matter and page layout differences. Haibun, using some of graphic literature techniques but shorter in length, would again need to adapt the characteristics to the tautness, unification and brevity of the genre.

birth hospital

inside too long   it will soon end

Architecture. Time warped. Hard work. Hard at work.
Arteries thicker. Torrents of blood. Flow busy. Harder
work. New colours. Old genes. Old furniture. New Babel.
Unspoken purposes. Unchange. Same. Built
stone. Mortar. Hewn fingers. Chisel and hammer.
Always busy. Too busy. Even small talk. All busy
for me. No time to view. Mural too large. Ants spread.
Efficiency. Together. Heads down. Concentration of
all. Damage limitation. Limit of roles. Necess-
ary. Essential to function. The function of. All
are wrapped up. Syncophantic music. All
unity glue. Heard. Unheard. A forever
presence. Ants silt up. Direction. No change of.
Impossible path. Predetermined. Unsteady
track. Disguised. How to complete? By doing.
On automatic. How else? Job satisfaction. This
meaning. Each their mask has. Each. Each Jew.
Each. Each Asian. Each. Each flux. Each
Flow. Seatide. Fish nets. Fish in nets. Fish
Jews. Fish Asians. Spike All. Squeeze all.
Barbeque smoke and crisp skin. Will to
survive. Each will survive. Will will survive. To
exist. Another envelope. Another posting.
Delivery. Successful delivery.
        Inside Relief. New face. Of purple.
                Redness. Lingers.
Fruit leaves. Fruit trees.   Separate.
Dependent. Joined. And Not. Forever connect. And Not.
        Pavement. Vantage point. Look up. Touchstone.
Conclusion: 'I' Here. Where propel she into Push.
Appearance of me. Ants propel. Ants spread.
                not too aware of
                but pulsing through anyway
                just this once

13

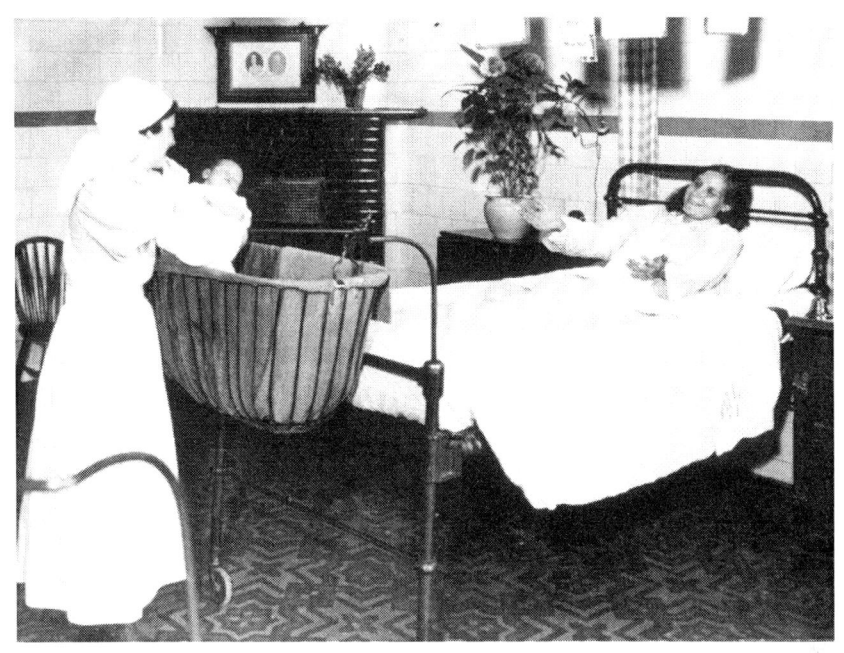

birth day

today. birth day. my.   yesterday. birth day. my. yesterday. tomorrow. today. my birth day. everyday. birth my day. you get it. you do not. does matter not. every my birth day every day is true is wonder day of every birthday that ever is. and shall be forevermore.

Birthdays are closing in, pushing, jostling, barging into ever shorter spaces of time. More space is squashed and squeezed out of shape. More time rattled. I deserve it do not. Happy runaway birth day, to more and more ancient me of rushed into future of speed. Rushes back to wish me yet another and another Happy Birth Day.

birth   days come   and go   in rush to   age to

age...   what age?

morphine in young eyes
cannot hear cries of the geese
or hack of dwid guns

I am 67 years old, in bed on a certain
Sunday, before a warning siren wails
through its piercing scale, before
another banal everyday-everynight-air
-raid-shelter-run, with no concerns
of sunset, ranks, backseat film shows,
and thoughts of war snuggling up to
less-one-leg-dad-from-another-age,
warm, close, peacefully tired,
secure in pillow innocence, all
really is safe and good in this
war-spread-eagled, scrunched-
up council estate.

sunny day
nearby the first bomber
prepared to drop

evacuee

1

Dad. Mum. War. Long way South. Evacuee. Cool warmth. Leeds. Mother and girl house. Clean. Roundhay Park. Nearby. Nighttime decision. 'Alice-in-Wonderland Daughter Flees London Nits'. Darkest drive. 7 year-old. Silent. Two giants. Sleepy disgorge. Quarter of Jews. Welcome to fresh of night. Welcome. Mother. 4 full-blown grown daughters. Big-eyed quartet. Fleshy. Lipstickey lips. Smiles of Life-filled smiles. Baby. 7 months old. Shares name. Daddy. Prisoner-of-war. Be OK! Mummy believes.

Fustle and bustle. Bed kisses. Bed cuddles. Clean sheets. No sewn-up tears. Every honey day. Shared between. Shared again. Passed around. Every bath time evening. Take turns. Give and take. Undress. Dress me. Undress. Hands of soap bubbles. Eyes. Big with feels. Accept my hurt. Comfort warm clean me. Clean evacuee warm. Comfortable. More feels. *his fears now safely contained in their all kisses* Sleep. Free. Sleep down. Sometimes dream grotesques. Always there. Close to. One or other. Love. Kisses out loud. Accept. I do. *i lay my head on pillow breasts a short sigh* Deep cleavages. Gaudy necklaces. Love. I do.

she and she hugs me
sideways glance
at their mother

2

Infectious illness. Spots galore. From nowhere to here. And everywhere. Mine. Hustle and bustle. Thin shadow spreads. Protect baby. Of course. Needs finger-signed. Distant family. Telegram to. Xmas eve's eve. No decorations. Of course. Rattle ambulance. Somewhere hospital. Sweat and sleep. Nurses. Lots to do. Rattles metal cot. No available other. Xmas eve. Speeds a train into night. *long journey a slice of moon first one side then the other* Sleep. Bomb free. Last of steam. Strangely destination. Her day unbends.

3

Xmas morning. One and only evacuee. Tiny stocking. My name. Mine. Presents. First ever. Father Xmas. Heard of. Came. Truly. To me. Night nurses. Drink my awe. Moist muscle and rustle. Broad kisses. Lipstick transfers. Night shift. Transference pleasures of. Yes. *with the dawn   ice melts   his sewn name* Distance. Journey unfolds. *along the corridor   her four part shadow   moves towards him* Double doors. Opens. Woman in black. Ankle length coat. Closed. Top to nearly bottom. Special shoes. Gangly shapes to fit. Black hair. Long. Coiled. Signature shopping bag. Cold floor. Nearly touches. Always. Bulges with London. Packed with ration book speed. Close. *young face finger painted with spots   christmas mask* Very close. *she arrives   warmth of silence   greets him* A heart can nearly. Unspeakable. Ecstasy of happiness. Thin-lipped. Smile. Widens with moist. Hugs. Inside and beyond. Kisses. Unspeak. Insecure jewish Mama. Kisses. Insecure atheist Mama. Maybe. Tears. You and your last born. Together. Christmas. This once. *Kayn aynhoreh**. Everybody celebrates.

> *in time*
> *2 boys*
> *blow up*
> *two frogs*

* *kayn aynhoreh* 'Thank God'. Evil eye is warded off. Used to protect a child or loved one. An ingratiating mumbo jumbo way into God's good books by thwarting demons and evil spells!

Venus

"Miss Pinkney, Miss Pinkney, I've seen Venus. It's HUGE - and VERY close to us. Come and see. Hurry, before it goes!"

"Stanley, I can see it. Is it really Venus? It's so red"

"Venus IS red. VERY red."

"You're probably right but I'm still not quite sure. Do you mind if we check it out in our Little Book of Planets?"

"OK".

i love Miss Pinkney. she loves me. she holds my hand as we walk past the school air raid shelter and into the library shed.

London slums

a drip falls
from his nose
then another

we emerged from the overcrowded
slums of London ~ world war 2
bombed us into george gissing's
'nether world' ~ fortunately we were
rescued from the religious fervour of
eastern european fundamentalism by
cutting edge socialist atheism ~ here,
there were no layers of interactive
family unions ~ we were on our own
~ complexities of racial intolerances
and bigotry, shared alienation and
brutal poverty, were resolved as best
we could ~ *where i come from,* alone,
vast numbers surround each other
with a common heritage of war weary
émigrés, continually being moved by
invisible people to new 'safe havens',
soon flattened, or in danger of being

flattened, by a new wave of those pilotless-propelled-tubes-of-explosive-game-of-chance, the V1s and V2s ~ it seemed *memorials are mixed* and we survived one near death adventure to be soon running from another ~ fear ceased ~ we were simply too tired to care ~ beyond that was the normality of chaos, the background barrier of relations far far away who, unwisely as it turned out, returned to the familiarity of the shtetl ~ america would have been a livelier bet ~ we all know about hindsight and other delicious clichés ~ if that wasn't bad enough, beyond even this was the isolation and dread of living with yet another kindly family when all cravings were targeted at mountains of love and to be saved hidden saved for them to bite the dust for this darkest of dark hours to end for no more brief encounters for us to stand head and shoulders above for me to paint the finishing touches to have it both and all ways to have the slate wiped clean and for them to bend over backwards to love to save to hide to save to love to love me ~ *blessings* and so it was written.

her eyes
eclipse the moon
she sees darkly

when i was very young

ration books
she was always
a bad cook

When I was very young skies were filled. Always. With fire smoke and gun smoke, with Spitfire aeroplanes and Spitfire bullet lights, with sounds, Barrage balloons and their ropes, ack ack guns spreading bullet tracers. Later were the new shape and sounds of 'doodlebugs', Worse than this, the sky, when I was very young, was filled with their silence.

snowdrop time   *but not where i live*

Near the sky, when I was very young, were the flames of burning buildings, the sights of burning buildings, the roasting sound and pains of burning buildings.

fireworks night   sky lights up   with bombfires

When I was very young these sounds above the earth were everywhere. It was different on the ground. In a camouflaged hospital the maternity ward and operating theatre spreads rubble. Splintered bodies, ruined bodies were visible. Sometimes, in endless clouds of dust, only bits of entangled greys remained.

where I lived   when I was very young   were no untorn sheets.

We borrowed a wireless, when I was very young. Youngest of a relieved, guilt-ridden family group, I, too, listened to the sentences awarded Nazi Party leaders at the Nuremberg War Crimes Trial. They were called out in the trained deadpan voices of the legal trade. I still shiver at the sense that, latent, hanging by a thread, was the possibility of a huge explosion from within a boiling cauldron of emotion. It never happened. Restraint was a necessary and effective part of the drama.

Tod durch den Strang. Over and again *death by hanging death by hanging death by hanging,* like a heavy line of blood-cleansed washing slowly swinging in a purified drift wind.

> *first day of peace*
> *i still do not know*
> *what it means*

Laughter was rationed when I was very young.

war rubble

hawks hover
no camouflage
in white fields

Twisted and smoke layered
she is war rubble.

His charred tears land on
splintered wood

sweet eyed girl
pins butterflies to a card
her impassive face

five stones

Do you remember how we used to play 'five-stones? How young we were.

We knew the parameters, and play and play the game over and over. As our skills improve, each group of five oO0Oos were thrown high and higher into the air. Each catch, each pick-up, is examined with a passion overwhelmed with youthful importance. We knew every success, every failure, would alter an aspect of our lives. Reactions, for a short while, modify, making a softer way of viewing each other.

I throw them higher into the air. Three were caught on the back of my hand. Two hit the floor and bounced in wayward directions. They point to an inevitable conclusion.

5 up-and-down stones
play the gravitation game
avalanche of sea

head cases

in our other life
dreams solidify
in this U and i
are masked animals
all glitter and dust

1

As far back as far is. Connotations. Images. Emotive. *'Mental Institution'.* Head Cases. Nutters. Intrigue and intrigued. We? Different? Similar? I? Discern connections? Acceptable? On a scale of? Which? Criteria? Whose? Points nail me. Blind dark. In a double bed I dream myths. Slay her dragons. Even wolves fear.

Close to. Spreading chestnut tree of poor houses. Explosion of. Head-case hospitals. Broiled brains. Boiled hearts. Rectified? Left to Die. Mum takes Me. Visit. Rocking. Mumbling. Shell-shocked. Nephew. Cousin. All day. Sits. All day! Minimal room. Rationed days. Bleak nights. She stares at his crangled face. Not the boy she knew. *He digs. Digs deep. Search beyond blue skies. Still curious darkly inside.* Perhaps. Nut house is forever. Locked inside. New outside. Other plays. Turn half round. Or 360 degree. Every three steps. It is someone's real. Wrangled clothes. Single person conversations. Non-visible response. Bump into others. Others bump into. No acknowledgement. No pain. Inside-deep-space-outside. Deep inside yourSelf. Exhilaration. Excruciatingly low times. Outbursts. Aggressive. Injury. Self-inflicted. Manic-lightness. Drug-dull. A world apart. Mum. Bit scared. Me. Akin. Alien. *Very* scared. Curious. Recognition. Indicators. Signals. Whose world? I need more! *Moonless. In your deeper black   an instant   imagination   in overdrive.*

2

half dressed
she sucks his cut finger
half listens to voices

Loot. Short of. Holiday. Job. Looney Bin. Fascinating dogsbody. Apparently. 1 day a week. Holidays. Specialist sicko's unit. Art therapist. Freedom to design. Be as creative as. Then. Few precious weeks. Hiding in patient safety net. Nurses Sign. 'No Weirdos After 9 pm'. Puts damper on. TV. Best time. Apparently. Extra curricular 'goings-on'. *nursey fixes drugged coca cola bottles   we slink into another world.* Study and compare. To know. More uncertain of. *A bucket and I fall past windows towards the sky.* A touch of shadows? Perhaps.

3

gull shadows   shapes crisscross playing fields   at speed

College. I right of. You left of. We more of. Not less of. Her arm jerks. Ghosts of rain. Intense bursts of. Highly. Energy: Endless. Enthusiasm: Thrives. Ideas: Non-stop. Rate of knots. Uncountable. Brainstorm: Uninhibited. Sleep: Less. Manic creation of: Obsessive.

Age increases it. Selfishly. Complex: so, minority interest. But such rich mix of. Left and Right of Brain activity of. No separation of. Every bit relaxed. Disassociated ideas. Fast to connect to. No concept of separation: Natural *is* connecting. Brain broils. Heart boils. Active. Simultaneously. Analytic creative. Emotional creative. No more division of. Wild outbursts of. Torrential range of outpourings. Ideas of. Emote to special awareness. No wilderness in. Control within wild of. Them Big Time Head Cases? No control of. Wild. Derailed. Not free. Yet emit vibrations. Strangely holy. Everyday temperament? *Variability.* Embrace. Make a fuss of. Yes. Extensive possibilities. Many solutions. Simultaneity. Think unthinkables. Many of. Must-have skill. Single problem focus. Single solution. No! No! Multi risk. Ridicule. Que sera. Hallucinations? Problems? *cries of a vixen   not even words in my head   can make amends* Downers are just as powerful. Just as dramatic. Just more dangerous. Apparently.

4

***they walk through mirrors   past reflections of reflections
emaciated smiles   infiltrate thoughts***

Effects. Not so noticeable. Why? When? Royal College of Art. Congregation of human similes. Even here! Most: desire non-aggression pacts, consensual agreements. Much talk diversity talk of. Unable to. Insider/Outsiders. Dislike: Disdain: loner loonies, aggressive behaviour of. (mild wacko's love). Their tidy screen. Carefully made. Distance from mess.

murky lake   beyond its darkest   stranger fish glow

5

Senses: Mashed. Stress: Pressure-cooked. Brain: Posted home via Chernobyl. Time to join in. Fully paid up member of. Alone and mixed. Difference? Not especially discernible. Except. It seems so. Same for them? Who knows? My Head Case – Good? Theirs? Close?

Not enough to derail. Not lose control of. Free up! Not lose control of. Vive la difference! Sometimes. Over-the-top in most of nut-filled land? Apparently. Backwards and forwards. Into and out of. Would not change it. Mum. What was she a bit scared of? Everyday. What of hers? Wishes to aestheticise. Anaesthetise their Everyday disjointed. Make to comprehend. Make oneness. Dearest Yahweh. Beneficent Yahweh. Allow Enlightenment to prevail! When? O Controller of All of. When will Unsafe unclean Unsane be cleansed? Abyss? What abyss?

struck by new waves   he turns away   from a tumble shore

6

walls kreeeek
as wee stalk thru them
winds blOwww inside

She also blOwwws bits of fingernails, swallows her nose and *turns off the light*. Mishmash. Illusion. Disillusion. Real. Unreal. Surreal. Parallel Realities. Beyond? On a scale of 1 to 3? NEAR END: Head-Cases-Of-Head-Cases. Extreme nuttiest of. Tragic appearance surrounds a next bend. FULCRUM: Much importance of. Productive of. Creative-Of-Milder-Nuts. Rearrange. Resuscitate. Reassociate. Juxtapose new of. More control of. FAR END. Everything-Else. What of I Me Mine? CrissCross. StriddleStraddle. Run up and down. Faster. Faster. Mad seesaw. Invisible door. Malaprop whore. Folklore. Always more. Never sure. Madder than mild. *Sometimes he lies upside downside - lets the sky turn*. Yet more. Horses for courses. Mine is mine. Triple trail. Dull to safe. Threshold. To my left: Seriously Heady Head Cases. To my right: Mildly Manic Head Cases. Yet not impaired. Productive. Verily. Emotionalist. Overy. Raison shapes. Yes. And YES again. Time to toast. "Lashes and Mentalhommes. Shake up! Take up! Snake up! Make up, until hubble-bubble spray over-runes; until unruly headshorn snipsnaps and hairesies coven the flore. Raid yore nu-clear dust-filled glossaries. Drunk to Mild Head Cases. And our serious kith and kin."

family portrait

bending down the stairs backwards i look up and see ghostly dad one crutch on the step above and one on the step above that look back down ~ one brother collapses behind a locked door tiny toilet room ~ the other tries to beat up mum ~ first i go berserk at him ~ with no telephone i then run as fast as I can to get the doctor whose disturbed breakfast feeds a fat ego ~ he will not come ~ above us the sky war goes on and on until so weary it collapses behind its own locked toilet door ~ no doctor in sight ~

hot-house implodes
debris of a vanished night
starts another day

democracy

nearly a lifetime ago i was taken to a meeting of the young communist league. i was young. i was shy. i listened. i heard the words.

that was the first time i saw U. i was quiet. U were quiet. i saw your big dark eyes. i watched U inside your big dark eyes. U smiled a small smile. i fluttered flushed and looked down.

everybody was kind. everybody tried to make it easy. everyone but U wanted me to join in.

i heard it again. i fix the word. d e m o c r a c y. i look at U. i say "what is it?"

Democracy   *just the word unhinges*   *different shells*

The Rose Hill Park School of Grass

grass between his toes
this is the start
of something
b   i   g

No Roses. Not a Park. Not like those beyond the divide. There is a Hill. Why not? That much, at least, is deserved. Time not wasted arguing the toss. Too busy not thinking. This is high quality preferable. Better than those endless rows of impoverished plans. Better than that rigidity of spineless structures, military repetition, cloned cubes, claustrophobic space. Better than the spine-crunching, lineal precision of planning department rubber stamps. 'No' to consult. 'Jerry built houses All the way'. Advert of an imprecise and graceless winter.

I knew it. You prefer precision. Right! To the left, facing downhill, shops, a sloppy foretaste of the Supermarkets yet to be; to the left, jagged outpost of a vast Council Housing Estate; ahead, uncluttered road, an urban bus route between here, there and somewhere.

grass shuffles	*grasswords*	*grass*
inside bloated books	*daydreams*	*he grows*
his growth young	*delay them*	*alone*

In a blustery age of flounder this happy secret happiness flourishes, an oasis of open-air expansion, a crunch of grass courted by an unusually early fall of leaves. Unlike later clatter and shmutter, Rose Hill Park is a confessional for only 3 years of under-growth confusion. Grass sounds make it possible to masticate optional language, be free to regurgitate OTT novels and absurdly paltry poetry, and re-adventure every morsel in line with closely guarded monitors. Here, at last, are grass desks at which I can write copious amounts of deeply conspicuous rubbish. Undisturbed, hidden from prying eyes, days pass in this tree-canopied, pleasure-garden-of-earthly-delights, imbibing passionate junk, writing passionate junk, lying, eyes closed, swallowed by tall grass, protected by stinging nettles. Nothing beats this unless, of course, you add an open-eyed-voyeurism-of-open-ended, way-beyond-furtive-couples who, in next to no time, abandon guilt, shame and everything else close to hand. With the slow sunset fingers forage with some success. A stocking twist, thin strips of flesh, tousled and ragged hair; they add light-flashing and engraved features to the stone-carved breathing of a demented teenager.

long grass	*her tongue and his*	*dress rustle*
it masks me	*coil inside shared lips*	*cheapest of scent*
from them	*no edge between them*	*drifts and fades*

At the end of each glorious, mystically fulfilling school day, when the atmosphere is still electric and empowered by gold dust, and the cerebrally imaginative is subsumed by more poignant elements that reside in complex, secret places, to emerge in forms more integrated and simple than even those of butterflies, the hill down to the urban bus stop comes into its own. This Mount of Olympus is where monumental opposition is overcome and numerous Gold medals, against all odds and to the ovation of lesser mortals, won.

golden award	*even more*	*blue shadows*
for a move	*blank sheets of paper*	*they lengthen along*
close to the edge	*doves float by*	*silver-lined clouds*

waiting

silent anger
when it cannot be explained
still he waits

(end of a long night   *start of a longer day)*

in the surgery waiting room waiting in an ill queue, waiting for a
doctor, for my doctor, waiting to unravel, waiting to see what face
she wears, to hear the pitch of voice, the shape of lipstick, the look
within hazel eyes, waiting, waiting for the latest cure-all, for an
impatient waiting moment when the incurable can wait no longer (it
seems ages the young doctor still does not look up) waiting for test
results (heart bumping along with undue haste so why the sweat?)
my expression an unperturbed mask, back cold with waiting, i wait
until waiting is over, but, in the surgery waiting room, waiting never
ends, (near the front for just a moment the circle closes) waiting in
a tight fitting, a tortured, circular queue, waiting, endlessly waiting

cornfield stubble
and a sky of ravens
he looks up and listens
as sounds of his waiting
begin to fade

waiting

silent anger
when it cannot be explained
still he waits

𝟙 𝟙 𝟙 ⬜𝟬𝟬𝟬 —𝟬𝟬𝟬𝟬𝟬𝟬𝟬𝟬𝟬𝟬𝟬𝟬𝟬𝟬𝟬𝟬𝟬𝟬
𝟬𝟬𝟬𝟬𝟬𝟬𝟬𝟬𝟬𝟬𝟬𝟬𝟬𝟬𝟬𝟬𝟬𝟬
𝟬𝟬𝟬𝟬𝟬𝟬𝟬𝟬𝟬𝟬𝟬𝟬𝟬𝟬𝟬𝟬

(end of a long night   *start of a longer day)*

in   the   surgery   waiting   room,   waiting,
waiting 𝟙 ⬜0𝟙 𝟙 𝟙 𝟙 𝟙 𝟙 ⬜0𝟙 𝟙 𝟙 𝟙 𝟙 𝟙 𝟙 𝟙 ⬜0   doctor,   𝟙 𝟙 𝟙 𝟙 y
𝟙 𝟙 ⬜0𝟙 r,   wai𝟙 𝟙 𝟙 𝟙 ⬜0𝟙 𝟙 𝟙 𝟙 𝟙 ⬜0𝟙 𝟙 𝟙 𝟙 ⬜0𝟙 𝟙 𝟙   what
fa𝟙 𝟙 ⬜0𝟙 𝟙 𝟙 𝟙 𝟙 ⬜0𝟙 𝟙 𝟙 𝟙   the   pitch   of
her𝟙 ⬜0𝟙 𝟙 𝟙 𝟙 𝟙 ⬜0𝟙 𝟙 𝟙 𝟙 ⬜0𝟙 𝟙 𝟙 𝟙 ⬜0𝟙 𝟙 𝟙 𝟙 ⬜0𝟙 𝟙 𝟙
𝟙 𝟙 ⬜0𝟙 𝟙 𝟙 𝟙 𝟙 ⬜0𝟙 𝟙 𝟙 𝟙 ⬜0for   test
results,𝟙 𝟙 𝟘𝟘𝟘𝟘𝟘 ⬜0𝟘𝟘𝟘𝟘𝟘 ⬜0𝟘𝟘𝟘𝟘𝟘 ⬜0𝟘𝟘𝟘𝟘𝟘 ⬜0𝟘𝟘𝟘𝟘
𝟘 ⬜waiting, waiting to be given the latest medical-cure-all, waiting for an impatient
waiting   moment   when   the   incurable   can   wait   no
longer.0𝟘𝟘𝟘𝟘𝟘 ⬜0𝟘𝟘𝟘𝟘𝟘 ⬜0𝟘𝟘𝟘𝟘𝟘 ⬜0𝟘𝟘𝟘𝟘𝟘 ⬜0𝟘𝟘𝟘𝟘
𝟘𝟘 ⬜0𝟘𝟘𝟘𝟘𝟘 ⬜0𝟘𝟘 my expression an unperturbed mask, back cold with
waiting,   i   wait   until
𝟙 𝟙 𝟙 𝟙 ⬜0𝟙 𝟙 𝟙 𝟙 𝟙 𝟙 𝟙 Ė𝟙 𝟙 𝟙 𝟙 𝟙 𝟙 𝟙 𝟙 𝟙 . 𝟙 𝟙 𝟙 𝟙 𝟙 𝟙 𝟙 𝟙 𝟙 𝟙 ᴈ . in the
surgery   waiting   room,   waiting,
𝟘𝟘𝟘𝟘𝟘𝟘𝟘𝟘𝟘𝟘𝟘𝟘𝟘𝟘 .𝟘 .𝟘 .𝟘 .Ė.   𝟘𝟘 .𝟘𝟘𝟘 ⎪𝟙⎪ ⬜𝟙 ⎪𝟙⎪𝟘𝟘𝟘𝟘𝟘𝟘𝟘𝟘

𝟘𝟘𝟘𝟘𝟘𝟘𝟘𝟘𝟘𝟘𝟘 waiting in a tortured, a tight fitting, a circular queue,
endlessly waiting.𝟙

Ė.𝟙 𝟙 𝟙   *cornfield stubble*

                                   she listens
                                   sound of his waiting
                                   begins to fade

MirAcles aRe forEver

secretly   they meet   Together they walk, not arm-in-arm or even holding hands. He likes her so much but has not known her long enough to be that intimate. He moves in front, unsure how she feels but wanting, and wanting her to feel at least something similar. *he waits for her   not feeling that young.* At least she is here, which must be a good sign, walking and talking, starting conversations and joining in when he abruptly changes from one topic to another. But who knows? Who *ever* knows?

nearly tactile

inside this unwrapped day

hints of nearly......

Gently, *dappled path   guides them to a warm glade   insects hum,* then up a soft-grassed hill, an incline that slightly shortens their stride. Close to the top, as the curves lead to one side she, now just ahead of him and breathing more heavily, sits and lies down on her back, legs bent, relaxed and open. Just below, he does the same before turning onto his side. From this position he can see her knickers. He spins their colour. Trying to appear casual, his eyes absorb their pattern, sinks into the shapes they surround. They still talk. His is fast, hers more desultory. He moves higher. Sun and walk combine to relax her in ways that make it difficult for him to interpret whether this is or is not a signal. Inaction is paralysis.

fingers nerves

slow intimacy

of a shy man

*He glances down   her thirties something cleavage   force of habit^*
Surely she knows he sees all that shows! Does she expect him to act or, being married, older and experienced in these matters, is this the response of a woman to whom youthful embarrassment is no longer a concern? He craves action. No matter! Act as if she isn't

showing and he isn't looking, as if she were not offering what he is desperate to have. Snakelike Eve and her tempting apple inside today's identity kit? Chromatic fervour curdles his calm exterior.

her body   in great working order   so many softs

Still he continues his staccato chatter. Simultaneously, in his visual head he tries to retain an image of an old woman dressed in rags with large warts on her face; anything that might return him to that simple intensity with which this heart-wobble walk had begun. But this is not a day when counter phantasy is effective. Even in top gear he didn't stand a cat-in-hell's chance.

painted face   phantasy rules O.K!

He tries to turn onto his stomach but it is not easy. He closes his eyes, hoping to drift into a softening semi-consciousness but the pictures remain, running riot in the film studio behind flickering eyelids. *He strains against   an old woman in rags   who soon disappears^* Bubbles blow inside a nearby dream of some other reality.

> *her medusa fuzz*
> *a shock of tight curls*
> *he breaks*
> *many rules*

Then she unbends her legs, yawns, stretches and begins to stand up. As she does so he hurriedly pulls at the front of his shorts. He, too, stands up. Turning away from the canvas of her intensely blue eyes he starts the hill walk. She catches him up and reaches for his hand. Heart pounding louder than the leaves they were crunching underfoot, he is ridiculously, head-spinningly, leg-wobbly happy.

they walk   from suntouched clouds   a surprise hug

Half way down she stops, turns to his dissolving body and, after a generous smile, kisses him on the cheek. Still holding hands they continue along the path. Nearer the bottom she again stops, but this time kisses him lips fused to lips. He now holds her, only stopping to regain physical stability. He drops to the ground. *unbearable waiting for her hands to rest on his thighs*^ Silent, she sits next to him, her breathing now very easy.

> *she fixes a teat*
> *on a coca cola bottle*
> *he glug glugs away*

They finish the walk without holding hands, without looking at each other, with no words.

> *secretly they part*
> *elated he cannot wait*
> *for tomorrow*^

^ *dick pettit and stanley pelter*

bedless

despair of the day
dissipates – water laps
a phantasy boat

It was during that first term at College and I was bedless. Don't ask me how or why. I just was. And, as often is the way when unthreateningly young, despairing of any solution and faced with sleeping on an empty, anonymous garage floor or some other bleak urban corner, help, in the heavenly shape of an always self-determining, always older, always perfectly beautiful woman, is always close by.

To crop an already shortened version, i was invited, no questions asked, to stay the night in her houseboat, berthed near Hampton Court Palace. Carrying my belongings, which include winter pyjamas, and with little 'i' clinging tightly to her flapping dress, like swifts we fly to this Nirvana of a solution.

Glorious epiphany of interior chaos and confusion! But 'Big Life' soon taught me to 'go-with-the-flow', sogowiththeflowiwillgo. But no flow, no completely non-metaphysical rush to blush can exist without the counterbalancing baggage of adolescent stupidity. Her married lover is on the boat, waiting with a smile and a cup of tea. What else! Although not exactly your stereotypically pristine virgin, I had only read about ménage à trois situations and, coming so suddenly, so unexpectedly as it did, am I ready for it? Can I cope? Who are these wonderful people, so unselfishly willing to incorporate me into their horizontal connections? Or has my viminal imagination mistranslated signals yet again?

Whatever the issues, practicalities resolved them. Encased in nightclothes, turned away from the slobber of kisses and frenetic thrash of noisy thighs, lying on my side, *I slept*. So tired from the swirl of the day's emotional entanglements, I slept! Yes, I did squirm as her fingernails hole my back, sweatily freeze at the climactic tautness of stretched feet and throats, guttural sounds and percussion bed, but I also slept, coiled in the warmth of not being bedless. Although not sure, my reactions seem only to increase their excitement. He enjoys supremacist situations, the masterful control of an experienced adult. She? Goingwiththeflow.

moonlight   yellows her body   he fails to notice

Next morning, tidily dressed in a suit and grey tie, content in his satiation and my lack of threat, he gives an over-the-shoulder farewell smile.

On my back, arms symmetrically held behind my head, and staring at shadow patterns rippling the low ceiling, I close my eyes to the close feel of her heat.

sunrise completes   irregular shadows   begin to stretch

Naked, she leans over me to reach for water, her face glazing mine. Surely, and listening for the silent sounds of what passes for heaven, this is going to be my day.

new man in her bed
even on the wrong side
it will it will work

holiday job

School. College. Holiday jobs. Way of life? Not really. Lack of money. Factor in way of life. Alternatives? Never considered. Well, almost never!

Languid summer. Scattered sun. I was told. Intractable architecture. Lower room. No outside inside. Low ceiling. Engulfed window. Intern. Encase. Imprison. Indifferent dead. Midday. First dead. He? Male. Large. Bran-flake skin. Scaly. Naked. Bald head. Hairy nostrils, chest, armpits, legs. Penis. Inadequate. Last midnight. Somewhere. Somebody shouts. Here. Newly silence. Nothing. No body moves. Nothing removed. Nothing stolen. They? They ignore him. Trolley? Pushed away. Me? Sicken. Sickly images. Of He? Upright? Very. Walks. Shouts. Hands? Move. Violator? Violence of Sex. Violent Death. Victim?

Reduce Shadows. Scupper. Non-mass. Vagina Violin. Scrag Colours.

23 more days. 23 more bodies. Death injected. Male. Female. Mix up. Stir-fry. Old. Young. Black hair, grey hair, white hair, layered hair, cropped hair, bluster hair. Legs, pubes, nipples. Shaved. No inkling of life. No smell. No sick. No pain. No images. No. Butchers concentrate. Cuts perfect.

Friday. Fishmongers' day. £Day! 3 pm. Card game. Serious. For my money! Cannot afford to. Returned at 5pm. Recorded. How rich would be. Satisfaction of knowing. How good at. Relieved. Just play. Serious. Dead? Ignored. Of course! Emotion? Save for £Days. Bluff game. Intensity of. Serious concentration of. Vials of. Me?

no sunlight
seeps into harder blood
the cold dead

Four chairs. No table. Trolley. Dead body. White sheet covers. Female. Pushed to room centre. Locked. Two there. Two here. 1 hand shuffle. Too professional. *5 of us   blank out her dead body   a 5 card deal* to each of us. Concentration. Card pile. Close to dead navel. Card slips. Sheet slips. She. Eyes closed. White white skin. Cleansed. No camouflage. Enfranchised. Maybe 18. Maybe not. Sheet slips again. Irritates. Pulls at it.

we sit

close to her dead body

cards reshuffle We play on. Concentrate. Tense bluff. She? Remains. Breasts? Small. Ribs? Pelvis? Protrude. Head hair? De-knotted. Matt black. Eyebrows? Plucked. Skin? Ubiquitous white. Unwholesome white. Pubic hair? Very many. We? Busy! Money? Small piles of. Her open hands? Retains some of. 5pm. Game ends. Losses returned. Thank you! Thank you! Relief. He holds corners. I hold corners. She re-covered. Taut trolley. Pushed away. Shadow-retched corner. Shapes move. Wonder. Turn. *solo with her   newly death breasts touched   until a rough scar* She? Young. Very. Age? Yes. Mine. Fragile? No. Vulnerable? No. *Her dead body. Thin secret, unknown to me,   also dead.* Suddenly cold. Body? Mine. Very. Shivers swamp into. Sick? Not very. Deepest breaths. Hands? Shake. Pantomime White.   Manmade light. Switch off. Self-lock door. Walk away. On autopilot. Holiday job. Paradigm of. Life. Way of.

Next? Years die. Then Dad.   Me? Sick. Sick of Sick. No alternatives.

Headmistress

butterflies
retreat into wings
a net of colours

She sits at an ornate wrought iron table in a railway station restaurant. Her chair, the same design, was uncomfortable. She would not be staying long. At the next table a model-type young man, neatly packed into tight fitting designer jeans, reads a letter. Lips closed, what he reads makes him smile. Folding the letter into the new creases, he replaces it in an ornately designed, paint coloured envelope. Then, looking up, he smiles somewhere in her direction. Caught off guard her cheeks transform into rouge coloured heat. Looking as if she were not looking, eyes slightly puckered, lips moistened, she sips her hot coffee. Too quickly, a single stick chocolate biscuit is unwrapped. Her lips combine to shape the centre of a blatant sexual metaphor. The tips of her thumb and first finger melt into darker colours.

her skin her hair   nothing the same now   large eyes larger

Rummaging in her handbag for a tissue wipe, she also reapplies unneeded lipstick with speedy expertise. She is beginning to sweat.

Far away, the faintest of train beats. Forgetting the coffee is tongue-burning hot, she swallows too much. Her eyes start to water.

far away
station music fades
an unclear song

Noisily, the chair scrapes the mock marble floor. With a wet-eye, somewhat gigolo and swift glance back at the model look-alike, she rises and, her leather case gripped firmly, softly exits.

her warm breath
the air between them
and cool swing of hips

Hospital Father

HIS SKIN HAD A SHRIVELLED, LEAN SMELL. AND OLD.
HOSPITALS AND PHILOSOPHERS STONE. THEY TURN THE OLD
INTO SMELLNESS. COBBLE TOGETHER AN ARGUMENT.
AN ARGUMENT FOR MORE MONEY, THAT IS. THIS IS A
GAME OF ALCHEMY. SMELL OF INVADING, INVITING
CHLOROFORM. PRIVACY CLOBBERED. NAKED AND
DISINFECTED. AND TALK, TALK AND TALK OF EVERYDAY.
OF KINDER UPSIDEDOWN. NIGHTS TURNED UPSIDEDOWN.
TOPSYTURVEY DAYS AND NIGHTS. *he looks* MEN
AND WOMEN WHO JUST DON'T. OF SYRUPSUCKING T.V.
PROGROMATTING THEIR SOUND-BITE POEMGRANITE SEEDS.
at the Star of David PROGRAMMING PROGRAMMES.
OVERDOSE OF EVENINGS. SEA SMELLS IN A DEAD SHELL.
HE NEVER DID BELIEVE IT. REDUCTION TO A MOST COM-
MON OF COMMON DENOMINATORS. PUNGENT SMELL OF
DEAD FISH AND WASTING BODY FLESH. QUICKLY
CAST ANOTHER. YOU KNOW WHAT THEY SAY! "A FISH A DAY
KEEPS THE DOCTOR AT BAY." *a twinkle of sky.* STILL
THEY WHITTLE AWAY AT THE WISPY SKY WITH SLEDGE
-HAMMERS. NUANCES FALL OFF CLIFFS INTO RAVENOUSLY
DEEP RAVINES. INSANELY UNREASONABLE CRUDITIES
LEAD THEM TO A BED DEPLETE OF LANGUAGE BUT REPLETE
WITH THE CHEMISTRY OF DRUGS. IS THERE A WITHDRAWAL OF REALITY?
OUTSIDE, DARKNESS YANKS ABOUT A BIT BEFORE RETIRING. HANDS
PRESS TIGHT AGAINST HIS NECK SKIN WITH ITS SHRIVELLED,
LEAN SMELL. *unrealised night*
topsy really is turvy
as seals toss tame whales.

Happy Birthday Mum

June 20th. Mum's birthday. 105 years old today. I made that up. Don't get me wrong, it is her *birth*day, but she died a long time ago. 1965, I think. Maybe '66. I must look it up. Only bones left in the ground, I expect. Subterranean earthworks probably shuffle even those about. I do hope, shuffled or not, it is only bones down there. Anything else just too awful….*even today   my fears   oddly fragile*

> *a firefly*
> *in the black sky*
> *its short flash*

Can remember her through the photograph. Sitting in dad's wheelchair. Lost her colour to a black and white image. She sits, small, looking so tired. Since about half way through his terminal illness, this has been mainframe. Her lifelong back length hair, soon to be shorn in the Hospice, is too grey; her third hand dress, still styleless and haphazardly spotted, too long; her National Health Service shoes, for as long as I can remember, specially built around her special feet.

She has just returned from visiting him
> *hospital bed*
> *silent she looks at him*
> *one last time* Buses, the start of
the Underground trains at Morden, changes, more buses, a walk – 'Home and Hospital for Jewish Incurables'. Can there ever be a more intransigent name, a more specific, plain speaking and down to earth description? *he is ill*
> *his last breath*
> *will be alone*   For a while I
worked there, a supposed 'punishment' for being a Conscientious Objector to Military Service. After his harsh first attack, to be nearer,

I request a transfer from tree planting and coalmining in Wales.

I stay for tea. I stay overnight. I sleep in the iron bed of a cramped youth. I bought a cake covered with outrageous icing. She loves it with a childish delight.

she still hides her tooth   under a blood stained pillow
hopes the wish fairy...

No one we know owns a telephone. My brothers sent cards. Two envelopes on the stone floor behind the stiffly open letterbox.

The one candle I found before leaving home, I push through the ridiculously bright, Walt-Disney-pink blanket of warm icing. In that tiny room, across the same small, rickety, knife-cut table on which we had our evening and weekend meals, across which we discussed, studied, questioned, listened, read, did our homework, across that very same table, wobbly but in tune, I sing "happy birthday to you, happy birthday to you, happy birthday dear…..". Quietly. Quieter,……and then silent.

eyes close   she makes   her wish

refrigerator

Dad said, "where I grew up there were no refrigerators". Mum never mentioned it. A troubled married life was also 'fridge free. Even after he died, even after I left home and that rampantly dismal Council Estate, even then, untroubled, she lived minus one. When survival was a silent priority and what happened to each penny really did matter, 'refrigerator' was not part of the language. Bottled milk on the doorstep every morning, there before we woke. Milk in a bowl of cold water was part of each day's collage. Cows, refrigerators and peace were beyond experience. They did not exist. Nor was sparse food around long enough to need temperature control. If a cauldron heat did ever 'turn' it, the smell would need to be rank, decomposition beyond recall, before slurping it into the sink.

So where did the idea to buy one come from? Was it a bold attempt to slide her into the Twentieth Century; protect an ageing woman from food poisoning; impress her with my largesse, the rewards of an extended education; make a difficult life more comfortable; repay her poignant love, this woman who had been taught to read and write by a man who himself left school at ten or eleven or twelve, she who licked the pencil after each written word, her eyes wandering? I don't know. Perhaps all of these, and that it was her birthday. Her life, beyond the doubtful gift of three sons, had been bereft of presents.

Buying is easy. With no car the difficulty is delivery. Buses, underground trains, and that final walk; all killers. Small but dense, it is awkward to hold. I arrive sweat drenched, pull the string-tied key from behind the letterbox and let myself in. A charge of adrenalin excitement as packaging is removed and the wires attached to a round pin plug. I explain it has to be left on for several hours to reach the right pitch of coldness. I show her the light that comes on when the door opens. I work the dial that makes it more or less cold. She wants the round edged, ice-white cube put onto a rickety table and placed against the wall opposite the window through which neighbours look. She asks how electricity makes a machine cold, not hot. I do not know the answer. She wants to know if the Instruction Manual has costed it for being on *all* day and *all* night. "No, but it is *very* cheap. Anyway, the other prezzie is this bag of shillings", months of slot meter food. She plays with the handle, rubbing its metallic shine, pulling gently in case pulling harder is not in the manual. It needs a strong yank to separate the thick seal that joins door to body. Hard won cold will not escape that easily!

she checks   and rechecks electric plugs   candle burns low

Eventually, as a warm day deteriorates, the moment of baptism is upon us, the 'Opening Ceremony' about to happen. She pulls hard at the door, telling me to "quickly, quickly, go get it". Slowly, carefully, gently, she places the $^2/_3$s empty glass bottle of milk in the middle and pushes the door firmly shut, followed by two confirmatory checks.

This is not a snapshot with a sting in the tail. Most day-in-day-out actions have predictable consequences and outcomes, and there is nothing visibly extraordinary about my mother. A month later, my next visit. There it sits, still in the middle of the wall opposite the dustier window through which neighbours look, still ice-cold white, except for the lace runner now covering the top. Her mother's. A cut crystal glass, again originally her mother's, retains worse-for-wear water. An awkward bunch of wild flowers staggers and flops in all directions.

When, in a tin kettle, she starts to boil up lightly brown water, I open her 'fridge to take out the milk. There, still centred, still alone, in all its transmogrified glory, stands the $^2/_3$s empty bottle of milk, a time-capsule work of Art.

a month inside
the refrigerator
going strong

Dsad. Fathser. Papsa.

(ghostly telegrams from a parallel universe)

Dad. Father. Papa. no way, ever, would i ever, ever, in each whole of everything, never, ever, not for anything, him call "Papa" ~ only notes, death correspondence, fantasies, higher levels of crumbling, would even drag out "Father"~ so, "dad"-it-was-or-nothing-or-something-beyond-any-present-a-nothing-and-ever-present"Dad"-goes-beyond-imagining-unless-*and-alone-with-rook-sounds-amplified-by-memories*-they-are-required-unless-something-was-asked-i-giving-up-early-on-any-other-every- connection, although, for her, it was "Harry" this and "Harry" that, Harry intimately Harry, unknown-in-my-inside-and-outside-and-through-that-strong, that-bedlam-gaze, in-close-up-hugs-she-pains-away-years, preserve of a two layered not mother, not mama, not even mummy, but a mum matriarch, she-who-never-gave-away-memory-collections-of-those-bad-sagging-at-knees-strengthening-years, and-so-changing-all-pictures-of-nostalgia, past-deadness-of-before-my-life, that is a past, past, past away, far, afar away, zigzagging away from horizontal limits of stretched actions, *they, a mystery of as-it-is,* no regrets, resistance, reminders, rebuttal and retribution, trying, eyes closed, trying, eyes open, trying to see back all that way back, to a page back page of beyond even his goodbyes to all that, *to disappear can time yesterday tomorrow no today, puff, gone,* to reaffirm sun torrid and sun of bright, way back, before Dad was dad, before, too young, 'signing up', army, Great-War-To-End-All-Wars, great idea, even before motorbike accident ruindown-rundown, military important message, so was it told by sister/mamma, and *imagine imagine memories beyond your own,* imagine againandagain, inventing routes, realigning to havens refuge, tumble-round-dingle-fairy-dell and cliffless safe, rewinding, re-evaluating split events, willing strong resist to them, a split second moment, *another-birthday ~ they-had-serious-doubts ~ about-his-next,* recover, repair, rebuild leg, refresh hip-and-joint, refocus-reawaken-rearrange-reframe-resplendent-life, where, over his body, she fingerpaints out all his fears, a brand of new man, tints of colour dissembled from scatter past bits, fragile signs connected by ones i can remake, massage, black-notes-for-a-sort-of-real-because-they-must-of-happened-because-it-is-impossible-for-them-not-to-have, even if built from scratch up, rebuilt inside exploding bricks, splintered wood slivered thin, glass shards, *make them happy days again,* shaped into a card house, where collapsing is no more a problem ~ sewn seam stitches invisible, reconstitution, refashioning is a hospital game plan, one played in each moment of nightday, where, what is happening now is now, then changes into changes of change, *relentless mystery-by some osmotic process-time knows its place* on and into yet more ephemeral presents and pasts, bake-and-shake-heat-into-happiness-again, happy-painless-again, replacing days many of overworked pains, he, Our-Father-Who-Art-Ill-Again-and-Again, learning-while-low-earning, He in whose name, in-the-name-of-Father-and-of-Son, melding, swallowing, 2 time-blenders into 1, He-who-strives-each-school-day-out-of-me, *i who live with fear always with that undercurrent of blame,* and-those-cold-scratchy-inside-him-out-shiver-tremble-ways-and-days, when-neatly-sweetly-snow-cleanly illusion and crisp dangers wait, settle into wet whiteness, a curvature of innocent looking masks, hot blood that would not melt a butter block ~

> *wide snowflakes*
> *they cover pavement cracks*
> *and each other*

preparing-for-sliding-rubber-between-neurology-and-sharp-end-wet-crutches of stable into unstable, upright to crumpled pavement fall to, *another-snowfall, with-misplaced-crutches, distance-slips* and, if it did, shadows spread on pavements and, inside, snow darkens to dusk ~ so-must-need-supporting-weakly-arm-to-so-bring-home-safe-and-him-sound-into-bosomy-heat-of-small-fire-sizzling-into-dank-of-room, today, always everyday, an-always-something-taken-for-granted-a-small-open-fire-in-a-compressed-space, opening up safety to, multi-functioning, unity to, that survives with little recall, once, maybe twice, a-picture-of-an-event-seeming-to-be-as-real-as-then, when, on a dull thirteenth, winter-sliced birthday, bus-stop wait for not this but next one, with him carefully crutching onto cracked, maybe, snow changing old pavement before a leg descends, and a yet heavier body,

purple-cold-lips
snow-covered-ice-covered-road
trips-him-up

before number 157 bus pulls local slosh into centre, clearer road, But remains not that much of *snow colours and a ravens ancient cry at dusk* before remains air raid shelters, earthy-rust-tinny *explosive night all our colours change from pink to white* and dad giving air raid shelters a miss, staying slumber in bed, playing Russian roulette with outside distractions and destructions, preparing for London-blitzkrieg-of-open-fire-hot-London-smoke haul, for tomorrow "to-provide-for-family" for whom that structure, that and every daynight, must be as it is in every particle of this world, a norm of norms, houses shattered, splattered, but-not-this-or-that-time-us, *in our shelter as another bomb explodes my young body sleeps* perhaps-there-is-a-special-one-off-god-for-us-for-surely-it-is-not-around-this-corner-unless-knowall-hurtall-and-powerful-granderest-eminence-of-all-eminences-had-it-planned-for-them-aeons-past-yet-so-before-even-past-was-past-every-present-ever-that-will-and-can-be-so-existed-in-that *long ago big big bang his particle friends* in-that-so-grandly-exposed-'moment-in-a-moment'-of-*that-greatest-of-great*-and-biggest-of-Big-Bangs-when-all-ever-there-was-and-yet-was-i-not-and-all-meanings-changed-into-a-convulsive-light, exposing our next at that and every precise moment from then on, and could not be eradicated but, at every one and same time, was no longer required, events happen, are no more but remain ~ *unified theory of matter is meaningless, it just is,* as is trying to decipher, lean on, take comfort from times now asleep, history is history, as is present as now and suddenly then, and subversive techniques against linear progression do include montage, and more ~ and why flee so completely from ruinous struggles of recall, rattles of one-time-long-ago-belief-in-overlapping-existence, my roles active, role of my spectator binoculars in every one and even more than even that, where are they now? what-remains-of-these-years? his-special-day-unlike-all-others-beyond-photographic-stills, his old skin copes, coldly copes, sadly-sad-depleted-sadly-defeated-sad-hair-thinning, it, too, copes, head-sculpted-gaunt, thickly prickly-pyjamas, ever-always-a-nightly-costume-shroud, alive-alove-with-conquests, wary-of-breath-tortured-inside-movements, outside-beautifully-formed, and-he-never-ever-wailing-in-manliness ~ what can and does happen? ~ *a butterfly settles on his pale lips another new face* this is it, now another living, different, non-judgemental, what it is, this old one beyond recall, beyond grasp, an incomprehensibly endless, restlessness, this-now-and-then-merger of-his-life-particular, fronting-on-his-death-unique,

he croaks   do frogs sing?

is impossible to know, inside impossible to be, his event, his transforming hours slow, pass slow into passages of those present whose watches slow and slowly stop.

she holds
his dying hand
firsts remembered

his real and unreal teeth hidden both, lost even, ears unnaturally unlistening, eye images no longer fat, no longer thin, accepting all that come their way, but, unloosening, undiscerning, seen in dustbowls of a distant desert, an impossible present, now certainly beyond any memory trail, even though bloodlines connect pits of pain to endless trails of exiles. It-is-all-that-remains-and-that-unto-this-day-of-each-and-every, is sufficient.

liquorice allsorts

he shuts one eye
more than half the moon
disappears

Did you know I get her single and married names confused?
Sometimes they just mix a little. On other occasions they completely
merge. Once they were a curious mix of undecidability and mosaic
that immediately unravelled into clean-cut alternate layers, like those
cubic liquorice allsorts. Mostly it is the names themselves. Which
name refers to which situation? It is there that the muddle exists.
like this night blackbird. I think it is seen, but maybe not. It happens
and, now, I accept it.

her outline
in an old mirror
a finger touch

sOoo0 bored

revolving globe

he shuts an eye
sees less than ½ the room

An element of the Course is called Common Skills. The aim is to
improve your skill in such areas as Communication, Personal
relations - both individual and as a member of a team.

Your final Diploma qualification forms part of a nationally
organized structure. It is recognised as being equivalent to
two GCE "A" level passes.

Workshops

These have been designed to enable you to extend your knowledge
and skills. You are required to attend at least the agreed
minimum number. Most students go to far more than this because
they realise how much benefit can be obtained from them.

sOoo so bored
she scans a window
and yawns

sisters

moons coloured halo
hangs beyond bright orange stars
she accepts it now

there **she** is, dying her heart out for all she's worth; and there is *she*, crying, shouting, pleading, making a right old hysterical stage mess of herself.

"Dora Dora don'tgo notyet youmustn't please forme". her face shrivels to sobs. "youcan'tgo notwithoutforgivingme and *passing the blessing*", a sibling enigma beyond the efforts of a mere son and nephew to decipher. with no gap for breath her rant rants on. "Dora you'vegottolisten openyoureyes goddammit pleasewipetheslateclean givetheblessing goddammit it'snotfair Dora wake right now or i'll go. Dora can I talk mama-loshen?[1]", and on and on until her verbal breakdown limps to tear filled whimpering that in no way correlates to the shaking she gives an unresponsive body whose long head hair, the pride of her poverty stricken physical life, has been crudely shorn in readiness for a tangle free funeral.

soon enough it is my turn to be spiked with metal barbs and grilled on the spit, no doubt thoroughly deserved by way of reparation for unconnected past misdemeanours like, when nine or so, peeking down the knickers of a compliant, ginger haired seven year old to discover what was so carefully tucked away. (Well, what do you expect in a family of 4 males and 1 very covered up mum?). one deep inhalation and volcanic aunt spits flames at me that, in line with parallel events of these strange times, actually seem reasonable. "It'syourfaultyou*could*havetoldmesoonerhow*could*youhavedonethistome? you'retoblameifshedoesn'tblessmebeforeshegoes*godresthersoul* Iwillneverforgiveyouandyou'llgoto*gehenna*[2]ifnotsomewhere worseyouungrateful*shlemiel*[3]doyouhearmeyouunkindsonofabitch." in face of this full frontal assault i defend by employing the 'deadpan expression' technique, continuing to sit close to the bed, still holding

hands with 'the-bitch-whose-son-I-am'. in this position i hope to achieve a state of dignified and cool non-responsiveness. *she* fails to notice. i retreat to the alternative, no-holds-barred 'fear-mode-Job-defence'. i am useless. insufficient practice. aunty wallows in nearly orgasmic hysterics. still, i may be getting somewhere because i notice her hair is rattled and her eyes frazzle, just a little. this is no joking matter but, inside, smiles begin to spread. eventually i try on a tiny, insincere "sorry" for size but, mutatis mutandis, already it is encrypted into the next generation code for "*Ihopeyouchange intoavitriolicbaboonandbecomepregnantat65fromthespermatozoaofan unspeakablyvilebeast,youhystericalnaggingharpy*".

she, in mitn derinnen,[4] opens one eye, views *she*, who fails to notice and, with what can only be guessed at as being a final act of familial defiance and control, closes it again. in that precise imprecise moment **she** goes and dies on us. my own mum, goddammit, just manoeuvres a small wheeze into her last curtain call.

40 years on *she* is still going strong, still rants, still suffers from that death-scene failure to be neither forgiven nor blessed for only god knows what. i've stopped wondering.

torn bed sheet ruckles
a committee of just one
crusts into old age

---

[1] can I talk mama-loshen?	will you understand if I speak Yiddish?
[2] gehenna	hell
[3] shlemiel	a simpleton; foolish person; social misfit
[4] in mit derinnen	out of the blue; all of a sudden

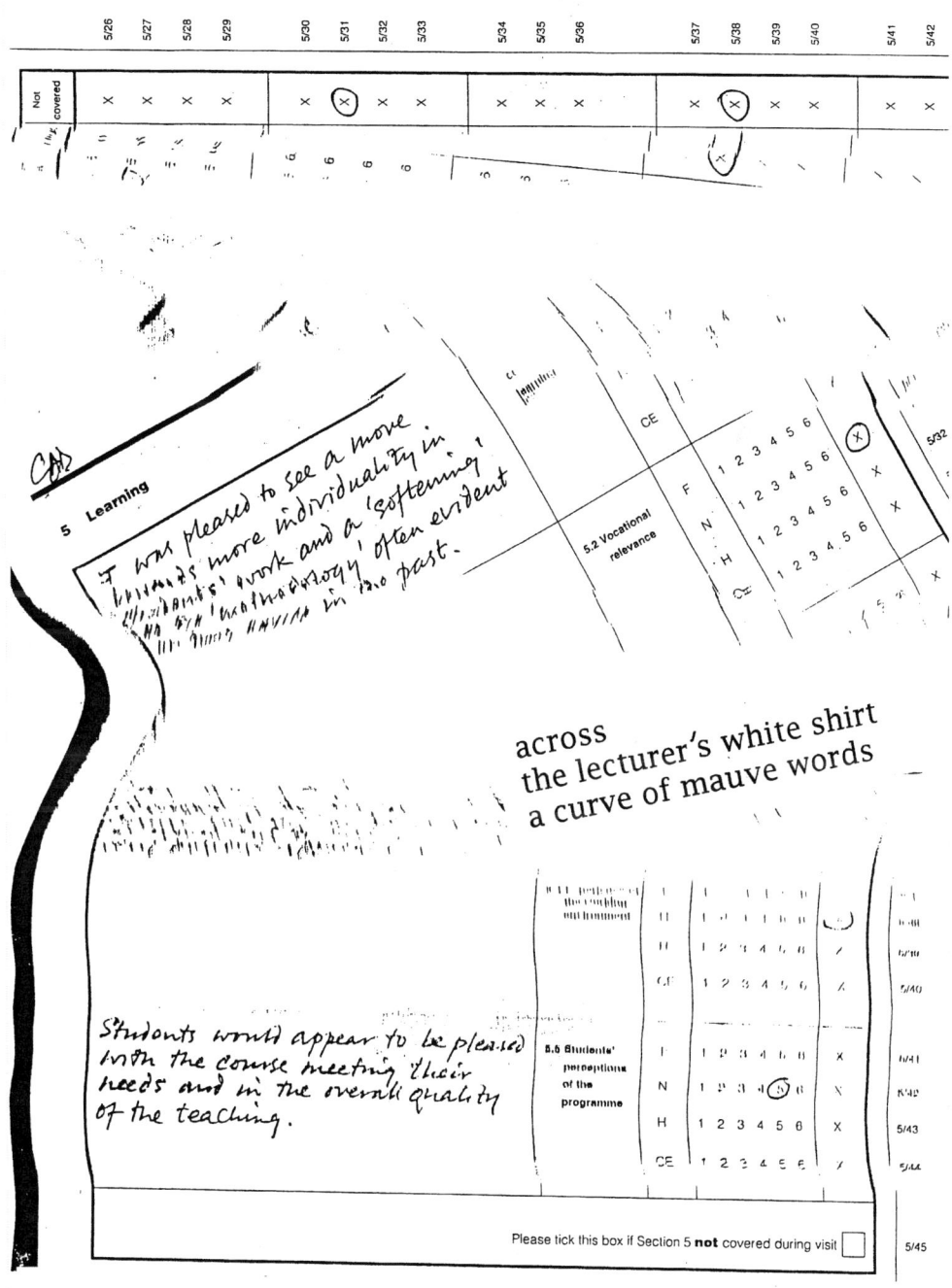

across
the lecturer's white shirt
a curve of mauve words

slow hazy day

a glance at slow curves
his sleep drifts in out and in
her new-found-lush-lands

It was a slow hazy day, a day most suited to sleepy meditation. Not the heavy stuff, you understand, otherwise it would not be sleepy. No, this was that lazy, that drifting-in-and-out-of-random-bits-and-pieces, typical of hotter days, when you lie on your back wearing as little as socially acceptable, arms pillowing head. Around you is grass as far as far is, on one hill, and then another and another, and this inside a landscape of mountains, herons wading through lakes, and pirouetting midges. On such days judgements are suspended, decisions quickly adjust to acceptable indecision, and thoughts are airborne the moment they intrude into such spread open perspectives. This was a day of acceptance, of weightlessness, of that self-contained irresponsibility which hurts no one, not even those you dislike.

she just hears it
sound of a white butterfly
as it settles

Here I was, arms folded under my straw hat covered head, wearing a pair of too short shorts. Nearby was an open book that had slipped fifty pages. No matter. I assume it also does not matter to the book although I can never be sure. Small dreamy snatches of events come and go, disconnected and unimportant. Ideas blow away. *canticle of dreams   rubbish floats inside them   as the wind stills* I open my eyes. *i shut them   and let the sun bathe me   again i conduct*

Great things happen on these nothing much days; a new head position, more irrational considerations, momentary connections and their instant undoing are not excluded. *sky filled sun   now too hot to sleep   a turn of the spit* This is a hot day, a hazy lazy day, a usefully useless day, a fragmentary day, only important in its soporific unimportance. This, then, is a day made from the very stuff and nonsense on which romantics look so gently, so kindly; a day wrapped in its own soft shroud, a dream, a majesty of a day.

As I say, it was a day suited to sleepy meditation, a slow hazy day.

> *pink day*
> *blue shadows change the shape*
> *of smiles*

bar-mitzvah photograph

1

Soft mists stretch along the harsh mountain crags. Shrill oystercatchers skim the surface of the sea just above limpet shadows. Further down the shore, on an outrage of rocks, seals socialize. Statuesque herons watch as wavelets slop onto them. Beyond is Kintyre, tapping into the tag end of a heatless sun.

A memory creeps in, sifting dust, seeping into pulp, lifting corners, irrationally spreading the past, ruminating on what might be the other side of patterns, on the converse of physical and palpable nature. A reconfiguration arranges the surface of this recall, half-truth, interpretative experience in which I now play a part.

Catacol – a small hamlet on the north side of the Isle of Arran. Seashore strolls start from the 'Twelve Apostles', a group of near identical cottages built in 1863 to rehouse the last remnants of the infamous 'Glen clearings'. Tenanted settlements destroyed. Replaced by more profitable sheep and deer.

2

When the invitation arrived to a second cousin's bar mitzvah my first reaction was to bin it. My second was to recycle it into a bookmark. Eventually, reluctantly, I accepted, and responded to the RSVP. Tried to retrieve it from the post box. Too late! When was I last inside a synagogue? Somebody's funeral? Somebody's wedding? That memory escapes.

Our tentacle of the family Octopus was not even Reform, let alone Orthodox. We were from that undeservedly ill-treated tribe of bad apples; not those that tempt flesh, but the ones that eat into the very heart of beliefs. Unnoticed, we practiced orthodox atheism and, just to add to the confusion, were as poor as the proverbial christian church mouse. The Papa of Mr Bar Mitzvah boy is a holocaust survivor. That might help me, as could meeting outlandish people related in some circuitous way. I knew it was an elastic family, but was this stretching my interior life just one imaginative metre too far? They may recall things I never knew; pass on elements of what I could never have. Atheists, especially those emerging from left-of-socialist-centre families, are, at thirteen years old, unable to accept the responsibility of manhood. They are outcasts to the minyan, not competent at any shivah. 'Purim' tells the world that tyrants and fanatics can be defeated, that evil cannot prevail forever. 'Pesach', the Festival of Freedom, celebrates deliverance from enslavement. These ideals even aliens can covet. The point is, I knew nothing about the ceremony to which I had been invited, and even harboured the nightmare image of second cousins playing some central role.

3

In pride of place, neatly set inside a swirling silver plated reproduction art deco frame, was the original of my chromatically modified photograph. So it was this second cousin's mother who was the facilitator of the technological offence. It was she who had spread the image, up until then unchanged for a century and more, across continents, in a sharply black and white disguise. Silly of me to forget! She fingerprints the family; to professor, shop keeper, college principal, charity administrator, Bnai Brith cousin, deaf niece, brothers and their children, to those who survived to live another day and just beyond.

From another place, transfigured, they are here. It is said to be an engagement day photograph. This, it seems, is what you did in those far off days. A special event demanded a special event. When the mysteries of pinpointing an extended moment, of capturing forever a part of what you were was comparatively new, when rooms of pastiche elegance were set aside and special décor invented, this was a newly established way of celebrating, a way of gazing, long after your own and even your children's death. Here they are, mutely centre stage, overseeing the entrance to manhood of a true and faithful believer, one of numerous unknown descendents. A great grandson is now thirteen. But who were they; this couple who own the room, this event, whose flight and survival dominates? The logistics of their escape, please? Was it horse and cart, dog and sledge, a hefty train that pulled them a thousand miles? Did they walk? Did they have money for the boat? Where could that have come from? Was it them or my father's parents who thought their journey would end in the hotchpotch cauldron of nearly catchall America? Who among them was diverted from Liverpool to the crowded East End of London ghetto? Can I ever know the answers to these questions and, if I did, would I transmit them at all, let alone accurately?

This browning, bromide-incensed piece of paper saturates the atmosphere. "He", an Aunt told me, "was a lay rabbi." "And died at 46," another said. 'She' I had seen in a second, small, time-creased photograph. White haired, she held the tiniest of white bundles, a baby, or something like it. "That's you, bubeleh," my mother had said, her chubby finger covering most of the space occupied by the photo. "And that's buba. Your grandmother". That was the extent of her family history. Later I heard she, white haired, was not ancient when she died. In this over-decorated room she was small, young, austerely beautiful.

I, who had moved far away, now moved closer to this time-suffusing memento, captured in a hold-your-breath-and-keep-perfectly-still elastic moment. Stillness, in those distant days beyond my possibility of memory, was a necessity. These were the parents, grandparents, great grandparents of many herded together for today's auspicious event. Their brothers and sisters and their families and theirs, may be standing close. On the other hand they might be that part of the family Auschwitz bound? Who knows? Were there secret pointers to unknown bits of the family? Fascinating, but even so, would it add up to much? Just another asylum-seeker family escaping a second-rate homeland for the bigotry and unfamiliarity of another.

Looking hard at them I felt disconnected, removed, unable to grasp anything of their world, their loves and despairs, their thoughts, their aspirations. Not simply a lack of imagination, of empathy, but a disability to transform a fading two-dimensional reality into three, now a book history. Even these are replaced by the more up to date *mementos* of the holocaust.

Although I pose questions about them, even though genetic similarities abound, they fail the 'electricity touch' test. Yet they are an integral part of that circuitous path back to Abraham and beyond and forward through me and on. I do not know either his or her mother's maiden name. My children do not know that of mine.

> he marries
> a kind and gentle shikseh
> his dead parents

They, through the diversity and divisions between parental lineages, can reject or select as they wish.

4

Where were they from? One Aunt said Vilna, another Bialystock, a third, a fourth, and the fifth, my silent mother. Perhaps she couldn't, or wouldn't, remember. Whose memory is the most accurate, or at least most credible? After the savagery of continual blitzkriegs, would records exist? Could they be found when if even the region was in dispute? Could it be anything more than historical nosiness? He may have run from the Imperial edict conscripting male Jews to an adult life of obeisant military service, or to escape the religious swords of Cossack horsemen, or even enforced conversion. Of this the photograph reveals nothing. Anthropomorphic projections are the only hope. But they must *be false!*

grandparents photo   cannot but wonder   how they escaped

5

His look gazes on the eye of the camera, dominating proceedings with features reminiscent, would you believe, of the Tsar. She, on the other hand, gazes away from the emotionless and powerful lens, as if to eyeball it would suck away a little self-control, some of her fragile but significant bits of identity.

Their pose, presumably for cultural reasons and technological purposes, is stiff. Faces emotionless, this, the celebration of a love intermingling, is an unsmiling event. Both small, their shoes had seen better days. The static pose is almost that of shop models. Their clothes must have been Sabbath best. Both seem neatly fashionable, covering all but hands and faces, he with stiff collar, she with a high-pinned brooch. She holds a stage-set posy between thumb and forefinger, he an edge of a studio stage-crafted and romanticised, temporary, architectural structure. Perhaps her waist is thinned in an early example of photographic 'touching-up'. He is wearing a thick, check-pattern suit. The jacket is long and, presumably, fashionable with its high, pinched lapels, slanted top pocket and five buttons, with only the top two done up. Is this a fashion statement, lack of social awareness, or just plain indifference? The trousers have no creases. Finally, is there something more underneath his jacket sleeves, his shirt? Another shirt, a vest, long johns?

The only sign of their closeness is her hand resting on his shoulder.

his shoulder touched to reassure   still he sweats

What, I wonder, did they do when allowed to move from their stiff pose? Did they shyly smile, hug and kiss with the pleasure of each other? Were their parents there, just out of shot? *that tattoo   a number stain on his arm   soap will never clean*

6

Yes, I know I am close to them. This never transforms into bits of her and pieces of him. Connective tingles are not there; never will be. Despite the surrealism underlying the photograph, and the unspoken role it plays in this day of organic continuity, they actually do seem suited, closer to each other than

I can ever be to this image-memory of them, spread fittingly across the paper, ready to face all their tomorrows.

It is inappropriate to continue the struggle. Even the starry-eyed, glossy and slippery effect of history fails to light them up. Today, in this room, another part of a distressed Europe, some other zeitgeist, someone else's angst, it is just not happening. This couple are being forced through me when veins and blood are unsure they can cope with the weight; indeed, whether there is sufficient heart to care. Curiosity is sated. I begin to feel the drain of boredom. Those people over there, dancing, with arms interlocked, and these others in the next room, all singing hatikvah, they may have the blood and stomach for it. What I gain most from this day of disconnected similarities is that adult second cousins, thank goodness, play no structural role in the Bar Mitzvah of 13-year-old second cousins.

> they shmooze together
> for what remains of this day
> we thank adoshem

The explanation is to be found in Pensées, pages 74/75, and indicates how ideas and concepts from one area of human endeavour can be in the arena of another, when appropriate. It is a Jacques Derrida concept of sous rature, which simultaneously cancels and preserves in order to indicate its unusable yet indispensable character.

What would we no-hopers do without that relaxed Lexicon, fount of erudite wisdom, and very funny book, 'The jOYs of Yiddish' by Leo Rosten, Penguin Books 1971. Thanks go to where thanks are due.

the lusting, the love, the one with no 'the'

Memories switch. Us framed. Freakish timeback. Themes. *smellingless cleenee clinical bo-dies tasteless arousal* Times to excite and frighten. With me to renew again for many times. Yes, me turned back upsidedown turned. You-me-on-top and turned. Tipsy curvy bed spins off. Back again. Moments of eruption and those to come. If I him were him or him would make no difference. Into our certain comes blind, blinding energy. *throat twangey   bodee at fever pich   inn that luv jungulair* Comes that forever unquenchable age. Day and night heartache. Pleasure-to-pain-to-agony to carousel. Liturgy. Of explosive days repeated. Hym-by-hym, sheet-by-she. Again turn. Fingers spark in youth. Yearn intensely more grammatical is than verbal to learn. *funtasty   is eazilee   mi beastir fantasty* and blurring limpet glue attachment & freewill is undone. Beyond out of decisions control. This begins of lifetime lasting. So seems it. Torn thoughts. Snappy feelings. Begins of everything blurred. Images mass blur. Multimode lovelust equations. Selfish, and so what, as *i work me tasker ever more wilderlee*. Broad confusion inside and out. Sea overlaps. We in a whisk. Inside creatures of lush days and nights. Yes, it quickly so becomes. Headly turmoil justifies holymess of crispy lusting-idea-of-love. Messy-boat-of-holes. Luxurious of inside fleshly and more softness, always in free fall mist. Schmaltz dribbles on another love Valentine's Day card. Kiss artists card. Ascending into handmade air, cheap scent floats. Again wonder who sent. Inside a joke? Possible? First touches of lips unleash passions. Head of pictures mix up. *off stage directions. she does not know his name   or he hers.* Muddled recipe. Erratic, insideout moments. Causes every curmudgeonly reaction. My youngness rides a bloated roundabout. 360 degree spins and flips. Never ceases to glorify. Stir me in, blindfold and tied. Repeats and repeats with always sameness of difference. *we caress her responsive pussy - breath grurrs* Conscience exfoliates. Miracle of a new blank sheet. Yes, work less now eminent. We, fast of dancing, entangle sweat of bodies to the hot of bed. But anywhere will do. This place, yes, as good as. Yes. Table. Floor. Cupboard. Ceiling.

Chair. Anywhere as good as. Throb murmurs of my and that body sinking. Clinging. Anytime. Anywhere. Bottoms down. Up. In rhythm, fingers secure. Tap time. *thrash of thighs and slobber kisses c'est finis* Ex-lovers under a bridge over nowhere river. Again curious, he deep searches. Under her skirt, inside softly, their manic response. Moving dominates those long ago, happy every riotous picture. *yung brests new his phantasy each and every way,* up to nearly now of olden, golden Age. Beyond blurred leans and learns. Sucker tentacles. Medusa search. Talk entwines head. Swop her for her, this mangle of fleshly emotives for those. Face colours change to metronome beat. Tangle of tongues when most tingle clear is needed. All control out of. Not used to. Unnatural. Rat tat tat of. Beyond tap tap tap logic. Every mystery refracts. Hers. Mine. More of her. Elaborate mystery. Drop into a crevasse that separates. New bus stop. She inches me away from. Groping at inside thin space between. Brush against. Sliver touch. Meteor glance. Taut throat. Door closed for business. Chitchat, chatchit of she and more she. Pass unnoticed. Slit space between. Brush against. Sliver another touch. Fleeting glance, and more. Relationships need luring from lairs. I a poor hunter. Snake curves. More agony pleasure more.

And when comes that day until magi breaks major dam in my way? Water falls on everywhere. Know not how and uncare.

I admit it   enjoy sex   minus love .   Unquestioning.

Accept. Giving. Taking. Uplifting. I accept. I do so accept its flows. *I cannot wait. Now not feeling that young.* Think to never of think. Hunger. Go grab with flow.   Unlikely to slow it seems in that thankfully open land. A spread in more directions even beyond that. Meanders in successive turns. Slides into curves abound. Full of large days and richer nights. Pump into wet. *we making mingles fondfeel and slonk   until funsets* Thrives on down-to-earth sweat. Humping and hawwwing. Grundling. Fast thrusting and faster. Anxious until fevers collide. Simple collapse. Total. Each breath heavy evenly softens. Until sleep and deep and sleep back. Until that samely rain again. He slips in. Links firmly back to love of sex. Drips she away. Tea, Toast, Sex and more she. And Chocolate. *gothic dress   tight to her body clings   fantasy wanders* Now not a no. Magic to look forward days includes nights. Unquestioned bits. I want. I want wild ecstasy. I want low insights and a mingle of maidenhairs. I want toward tension. I want mystery of half hidden. Her diaphanous slip. It excites. Room shadows soconnected theymerge. Still time for bodies to shape shuffles. Still time before bath share gives new angles to squashed flesh.

2

newness of every moment present he nearly she loves with this now seemingly special Her who nearly slips on an illusion of mirror images he and I reflecting acceptance with no questions asked delirium. join up to merge a next illusion of love with sparks of descending kisses that astonish inbetweenitees with little of love but frictions of gentle effort in a coalgold seam of what seems love inside nakedness over many years of same pressings same sights special soundings mostly tasty like that of furry apples like synthetic snow like overripe slightly bitter of taste that still responds better than sweetly sugar candyfloss and *whispery softung   lickerlings and othersongs   around her bushyflesh* cling of clinging and clingfilm creases on faces with a suffocate of sea lap dreams that drown again in fingerlings again to wild abandonment of decorum taste and unaware of anything in control of those living bits beyond her libidinous welcome uninsight and care not we who finds space there or hide behind thickets or lie park bench sandwiched even and nude be seen and naked on warm swish around grassland or press uneven tree bark even being watched do not care for heavens sake we who are out of control *play grabbatty games i sing a finglecumble here and a tingle there* in a messy fleshy mass of who did what to who in how did what with no questions asked of why did what to wet lick wallow and swallow out of control from those who hide and seek watch and next to me you sing and next to her i sing a music bejewelled made-to-measure song of lustings-in-luv not wanting to know whys wherefores and did I not make senseless songs of remembering andhappier for how long then wanting what and why so many times in heat beat heartbeats along a stream of hot breath. In his head her beds seem to bleed. Breathe in some parts of some other one's breath. Scatter inside someone else's bed of ground cover flowers. Roast on a spit. Slide into somebody else's summer space. Holes crack. Get used to endless. Love becomes of physical. And beyond? What? No to questions. No to more cerebral? Again on wrong side of bed.

> *ineptly*
> *she combs his hair*
> *he wants her to stop*

Queues of flesh squish in sounds of knowing we can. Wilder happy of happy. Out of breath laugh. Ruffle crimped hair. Blue eyes. Or not. Learn to clever with laugh. In touch with necks and necklaces, rings and other teasing accoutrements of midday play. Naked to body towards a love ride imminent. MaskKissMask. Chocolate loving years of. Smooth, creamy, dreamy years of. Thoughts of She never ever cease. Never end. Collage of She. In every direction, sharpest of sharp shadows. Fades spread. Still sharp centres until away and away sun moves. *Touch of her. Wind stretches. A moon soaked night.* There they go again, slurring into yesterday. Repeat pictures. Imagining dreamsy again bits and pieces. Kitsch brightens again fluffier bits, schmoozes over grandiose feelings. Never enough again times. Again pretend of loving lovesy dovesy loveliness made intensely for schmucks sake. And then to bedding madly crumpled again. Nowhere calm. Madness. Gift-wrapped parties pump toward olden times. Look back on rich pickings. Insecure youthflings. Succulent love shadows. Wet day's diversion. In shared beds, we listen to them hump and schlump.

> *with little passion   i begin to rub   softly flesh dry.*

Not blessed with best of stereotypes, other machinations, devices, concoctions, twisting and turnings make connections toward each new delicious. Of sadness? Have that for me no more. No, not for me, thank you very much more of this and great, grave secrets will out and about. Our secret no more. Involves: Different day talk. Special night of talk. Upgrading entertainment. Make-you-a-laugh. Attracts Yes responses. Yet more intensity talk pleasures to her desired creatives-vanity-ideas-urges-fantasies-upgraded-and-achieved-for-head-and-heart-of-her. *Always* a winner! Always a bed arrow flush with blood, blinded in petal scatterings of much feeling *this* is love, this *is* love, this is *love*. No mirage this. Coveted in such heat of desire, real and not is hard to deal with. Can shadow distinguish from owner? Suchtouching closeness. So close nothing of space can seen between, indistinguishable from those born on a gold chest of between his ease and body of she perfect.

Sea change between bodily gorgeous bodily inside mildly mind. Sorting it out. She, in slinky dress redesigned to cling to my senses heightened. Tread carefully. Very. Outside, feeling inside with care. Senses stretch, rubbing a merger with moon-glow. Thrones become muddles of maybe this or not even that. Gradually, lusts reign less supreme.

on her birthday   they kiss and kiss   moons corona

Gloriously mixed messages gorgeously dissipate. Much unsure but edging close to. Where? Where there such love thing is for sure. Uncertain how. Certain I may be no one knows for sure. Yet inside many nights of inside days, a somewhat trust begins a journey tossed up, or so much of it surely seems. *she licks an edge   where his lips touched still tastes of him* Mix of other less expressibles shifts some warmth. *dusk again and cooler colours on your lipstick* Understandings beyond even that open up. Above and below sensations. Releases me from creased clingfilm. Closeness unwraps freshness scented. Inside, my unrelenting obsession. U, an addiction. Childish of still intense of jealous of losing her to other vibrations. Due a clean-up review. Extensions of smell, of time-to-grow-is-upon-me.

Still. Mergers of fleshly inside even my female bits transform other possibles. Believing in a one love onto another, and not all understanding how and why of this new. Luck plays upright part. As does upright piano and other music. Planning, too, of bed bumping attraction, and more. Her skirts still rise, still fall. Fleshly curves still smile around fleshly desires. Yet can now extricate sheer pleasure from straitjacket. Rarity luxury of surprise. What fortune great and good to meet on this easily caressing carousel, slide off and move on to U other parts.   *i follow   your curves   U let me*

   Mattress of grass visions mingle blatantly exotic smells and with season precise herb and spice tastes. We close rest each other. Watch humming bird silences. What is happening and wonder does it beyond and can it further go? Ingot questions. Inside snow-white comfort ad hoc rules prevail. Now and here distinguishable from events time-polished, sparkle-coloured by memory-like-somethings. Room for space between again. Slits and crevices again. Mystery of she, she and she at bus stop of long ago blushingly uneasy time. More mysterious fluid. Unshamed passion. Unashamed flux and fusion unreleased abounds. Every soft day high-octane. Soft confuses and flatters. Close to less uneasy. Disordered playing card pack. Unpredictable order easy and complex. Aspire from unquenchable lust Age. We meet. We merge. Is there more?

perfume
in the air
i&U

BHS

**BRITISH HAIKU
SOCIETY**

Contact Maggie

*more interruptions
he tries to hold it together
but fails*

MANAGEMENT COMMITTEE

*again upset
again looks away
from the book*

Meeting : 2 pm Friday, 27 September, 2002. Diawa Foundation Japan House..

AGENDA
SP – chair

1.   Apologies. - *CA*

*why not an anthology?
BHS members in B/S.
1998-2002.*

2.   Minutes of Previous Meeting and Matters Arising. *– too many inaccuracies – why SO late?*
     Meeting held Friday 28 June 2002 at 2.0 pm - Diawa Foundation, London.

3.   Treasurer's Report : Chris Allinson.
     a.   Signatures for Barclays, Charity Commission - update.
     b.   Sasakawa Jury Fees - update..
     c.   Haiku Literature Award - update
     d.   Current Finances..   *£457 current account   Sep/2   Rep £752
          £1359-22 current A/c.   – £500 retransfer
                                                              A/50 histor...
                                                              £ landship*

4.   President's Report : David Cobb.
     a.   British Museum Haiku Book - Publication update. *– great draft!*
     b.   ' Brushwood' -Haibun Publication, Nobuyuki Yuasa Contest - Report. *Quality production – NOT good*
     c.   ' Arrow of Stones" by Ken Jones - Sasakawa Award Publication. Update. *EGO! EGO! EGO!*
     d.   The BHS silver drinking vessel- presented to past President - a proposal for discussion. *Someone – in this context*
     e.   W.H.A. Conference - Request for Support. ENCLOSED COPY.
     f.   *The Blue Plague Story – re Blythe – rejected*

5.   Journal Editor's Report : Colin Blundell. *– Number of members?*
     a.   Blithe Spirit Vol. 12 Number 3 - September. *Suggestions*
     b.   Colin's August Weekend: *Momentum of Haiku Cal. results or Press collecters or competition
          e/ No meeting of Tanka Splendour Comp. re Alison Williams*

6.   Newsletter Editor's Report : Stanley Pelter.
     a.   BHS Rules - discussion. *→ different agenda items !!   HSA Journal*
     b.   To meet, or not to meet ! Discussion. *too much reliance on e-mail non-contact contact*

7.   Events Officer's - Report : Brian Tasker.
     a.   St. Cuthberts BHS Hike August 02 & 'A day at the seaside' event.
     b.   AGM Nov. 23 - Events, workshops etc.
          Spring Conference 2003 - Venue. *(table)*

8.   General Secretary - Report : David Walker. *– why Vista SO loud!?*
     a.   AGM Election of Officers - General Committee Members, Update *be given previous 2 yrs attendance
          if small - (As we have two vacancy. Who is
          present Comm. tee will be stood). No one knows
          our attendance record.*
     b.   Writers' & Artists' Year Book 2003 - Published. *£13.50
          £8.00 /year*

9.   Public Relations : Jonathan Buckley.
     a.   BHS Website - update. *Survey results very variable!!!*

!!? us/   *A.O.B*
     Date and Venue for Next Meeting.   Diawa House - Fri Nov 22 at 2.0pm prior to AGM 23 Nov.

Anthology.   Members Handbook

day trip

she looks
at his crangled face
her arm jerks

On the way home, just after a sharp bend, we stop in a lay-by. It has been a hot and very long day. The windows are open but we still sweat. On the other side of the hedge is a field of sheep. Before we can reach for the wet towels, before we can find the box of cold drinks, before we can even relax our breath, he is out of the car and through a gap in the hedge. Hot as we are, we get out as fast as we can and scrabble along the bank, trying to find a gate, a hole, any way in.

sheep bleat
across the field
underground cables

We can hear the kafuffle, the overarching, insistent barking, and the loud, interrelated sounds of sheep. Even knowing his response was beyond his control did little to abate our feeling of powerlessness. When, eventually and heavily scratched we force a way into the field the picture is, gratefully, not as feared. *corn stubble   a van gogh sky* There are no dead or even injured animals; just a chasing down, a swirling and swerving group. We, too, re-form.

> *sound of our breath*
> *edges jigsaw*

We call loudly and repeatedly, but are ignored. A man with a gun is also shouting.

> *we look across*
> *shout*
> *he looks across*
> *shoots*

We run forward, still calling. Another shot. He drops into stealth and fear mode, slithering through grass towards us. At last I can grab his collar. Sweat runs down everything. I carry him back. Dog first, we push and scratch our way through brambles and into the car. Hot, windows closed, without a word, I drive away.

> *fallow field*
> *a little adventure*
> *fails to complete*

huffypuffy

huffypuffy, menstrualmaletensioncrotchy, overthetopstroppy, blindmindedlygrind, gruffandrough, mentallystripstrapped, sharplystropped, scrumblerumblecrumble, fullybully, blackseedgreedy, and then a ghoulish lord-protector-of-the-morals-of-those-who-do-not-ask-to-be-protected-but-will-be-protected-whether-they-ask-to-be-protected-want-to-be-protected-like-to-be-protected-need-or-do-not-to-be-protected, smashrocksontheweak, seentobemean, greencreambloodandscream, tough-looks-as-if-he-has-to-be-a-highly-moustachoed-stuffyairman who-can-and-does-huffandpuff, pushandshove, puffandhuff again, louder, and then even louder, until there is nothing cello, nothing mellow, nothing soft, nothing round, only-rebuttal-nothing-subtle-nothing-restrained, nothing, nothing, nothing but more gravellyhoarse left in hollow**bellowland,** in courseunland, unbirdlessplan, whiteknuckle-in-tightfisthand.

Above his huffypuffy waistline he shakes and breaks with the effort. *Below is more scary;* levels of tattletale, tearsoakedtales, fullscaletelltale and failtrailblindwellbeing.

> *well I never!^*
> *did you ever screwball*
> *you puffball man?*

Never ending, her fumbling lovebirdwords tumblestumbleandrumble, humblyslumble over the dipping and diving, foaming and lurching, twisting and thrashing watermill.

> *a shy look**
> *in a Victorian nightgown*
> *back in fashion*

* *dick petitt*
^ *dick petitt and stanley pelter*

Passacaglia *Fêtes Galantes*

In Scotland it is in Nottinghamshire; in England it is not. A sign colourfully states: *'Gateway to Lincolnshire.'*

Once dedicated to St. Peter and St. Paul, for reasons time obliterates, the church in Claypole dropped St. Paul. Sufficiently ancient to be mentioned in the Domesday survey, inevitably the original wooden Saxon church was rebuilt. Today it still confirms and solidifies the faith of a dwindling congregation. Not belonging to this butter group it is neither my social centre nor a fear support system.

In an unusually soporific vault this evening's concert play the work of Joseph Bodin de Boismortier. He was prolific, and successfully cross-fertilised Italian and French styles and traditions. Melodies were concise with imitative dialogues. It worked! He was popular! An eclectic programme, it is performed by the homely Passacaglia Quartet, consisting of Flute, range of Recorders, Viola da Gamba and a Harpsichord lavishly painted à la Italianate Watteau.

a   1   2   3   4 -
recorders in harmony
filter church air

This is not sacred music. Secular background to a turbulent French musical and social scene, it reflects a period when the rich could *become* their extravagant parties. Held in private gardens of private homes, a temporary mask of transference covered their lives. 'Dressing down' for a short exciting time, with no fear of hunger or impending danger, they copied and enacted a pastiche of their peasant workers and tenants. Lots of fun before clambering back through their Rococo-framed mirrors.

a pair of ravens
swoop through their conversation
ornate reflections

An interval. Miss wigglebum sitting next to me leans over my sketchbook with an innocent directness. She compares the drawing with the instruments left in positions of angled order. Had she failed to see the space between Viola da Gamba and floor? The evening package includes a drink. I move to the door of carved panelling, tracery and handmade nails.

½ way through

       an evening of bright music

              a yesterday voice "Stanley Pelter?" 'If I had a pound', as my mum used to say, 'for every time I've heard my name spoken as a question,' and that instant fear of failing to recognise the person within the voice, 'I would be a rich man'. Beyond the contemporary hairstyle, fashionable, smartly expensive dress, balanced, tasteful shoes and mature make-up, is a flashed recollection of a forgetting. Familiarity at a distance.

> *her neat smile*
> *fills with planned colours*
> *blonde hair streaks settle*

She seems more beautiful, more together, more in control than someone I would know in that far-flung centre of an overcrowded and disabled memory. Something structural vaguely reminds me of the different person she used to be in whatever part of my life we inhabited together. She does look good, exuding a remote touchability. I want to, but do not. "Sue Archer. I used to be Sue Mount." My face, suddenly bustling, curls into a masked smile of recognition. "I'm still in touch with Jenny Rapp. You remember Jenny, don't you?"

Now here was a skinny-dip swim in a far-flung lake. For a time Jenny lodged with us. We had a number of Butler-led, Waitress-fed dinners with her parents who, spread throughout the evening, gently probed for anything that might hint at drug-related experiments. Their, well, mainly sober daughter? It is one of natures curiosities how different parents deal with such concerns. For a time, Spike Milligan phones daily, obsessively enquiring into the welfare and well being of a daughter, temporarily stationed with us. Polite, direct, always serious, it hid a neurotic need to know whether, with magic powder, I am protecting her from a hyperactive drug scene. I hide behind fluffy, establishment 'student confidentiality'.

Retrospection inspired by this flashing light from an exciting past fails to halt the machine gun fire of questions. Asked so musically the abstract sounds are more pleasurable than the content. "Where do you live? What are you doing here? Are you….?" "In this village, here, in Claypole. And you?" "Not the next village but the one beyond. Brandon. I've a son. Starting an Art degree course soon. Chelsea. Divorced now. And you? You visited me in that god-awful College, in god-awful Stoke-on-Trent. Why did you send me there, of all god-forsaken places?" "Well, at the time, for the subject you wanted, in the way you wanted to study …."

"Please take your seats; the concert will continue in 2 minutes." Just time for a telephone number and address before the interval finally collapses. Without looking back, sweating a bit, I regain my front pew seat; next to Miss wigglebum and her looking-as-if-she-wants-to-talk-to-me mother. I give a shorthand smile and open my keep-me-private sketchbook at a clean page. 'Sonata in D Major op 91/1; Pièce de Viole; Deuxième Livre and Gentilesse op 45/5 in G Major'.

musicians death mask   inside a transparent box   his music silent

By the time I am ready to leave, she had gone. I cannot tell you what I remember about her.

ccoommiitteeee mmeettiinngggss

ccoommiittee
mmeeeettiinngggss
rreeppeeaattss rreeppeeaatts rree

ccoommiittee
mmeeeettiinngggss
rreeppeeaattss rreeppeeaatts rree

BUSINESS SCHOOL MEETING 2nd May 4.45pm Camberwell centre
CREATIVE SCHOOL MEETING 3rd May 9.30 - Surrey Docks centre
SCIENCE & TECHNOLOGY MEETING 3rd May 5.00 - Waterloo centre

hiss of rain
reality & illusion -
1. Differences between ~~████████~~ HoSc ✗ guttural sounds

from his throat
2. Strategic Plan

'To serve the corporate mission of providing a broad vocational provision
meeting the needs of the communities we serve across London and beyond
and providing clear progression routes for all our students'.
= WOW! *a dreamboat of a mission statement.*

3 Costing of Courses (see attached sheet) ·

4 Parameters within which we must plan *again*

(think of some surreal activity traditional lingo to '133 up meeting's !)

a Unit target: Creative : 64617
Business: 46568
Science: 44299 (excluding A/level - GCSE)

b 16hr rule: Part-time students *guided* learning hours

d Staffing levels and expertise — *too low and not good enough.*
→ *been here before, & what happened to them*

5 Ideas from staff - chaired by HoSc ! !

Look at groups *of courses*
Not individually.
re . cost effectiveness

far away
a Bach cantata
their raised voices

cannot function.

policy re . retention

we say we are student centred but....

84

A Small Cheer For TV

I watch TV. It informs and enhances whatever else I do. Not the quality of the print, you understand, or the point size or typeface, but for its inherent nature and how it goes about its business. A Premier league 'backdrop' invention, it is effective just in being around, a positive aid to provocation. It fits need comfortably, like an expertly made-to-measure glove.

when coverage is each minute of every 25 hours eight days a week 53 weeks a year year in year out everything and nothing is made important. every/war minutiae is treated as if of equal importance, no less than the severity of the second world war endlessly repeated. real time is encapsulated in tv time and so without our agreement let alone awareness we learn a new time. tv timefillingquestions to 'embedded' journalists embed into timefilling backgroundinanity. likewise the proliferatingawardceremonies. the live activity for expectant and excited participants their years highlight. we watch the narcissistic illusion that is tv. *opera thrills sailboats, a marvellous ad whatever it's for** we see and listen to their decisions. rationales are a private social nicety. my fee is for backdrop and that is sufficient. rarely do i want to be involved. involvement is not what is important about tv. with the exception of *athletics, football* and perhaps the enticingly badly acted, caricatures-to-die-for, hooklineandsinkersyou soapopera *eastenders,* little is retainable. and even if this is exaggerated, so what! tv TV **TV** does it all the time. and i I **I** am an obedient learner.

tv
it is and is not
real

the point of tv is to facilitate primetime highvaluetime thinkingsensingfeelingtime fargreaterthansilenttime. *take a break the magic ingredient   will change your life^.* this is the environment that enables ruminations realisations outcomes to not only thrive but be qualitatively different to anything emerging from any other background. far from being neutral it has underestimated powers to both blank and enflame reactions. sure it is additive.

i perskerate
me plonker
now with strider strokes

talking of *now,* now where could *that* have come from if not tv. so just what *is* this *plonker?* (not to mention *perskerate).* sure, the everyday word for anybody setting themselves up, sword in hand, as protector of our wayward morals is *penis,* or some such thing. tread carefully, we're talking haiku here! subject? content? context? the appropriate word? callaspadeaspade? do we? dare we? should we?

valentines day post   *she does not believe*
rubber genitalia   *in calling a spade a spade*
the shape of a rose   *never ever wanks*

Dear oh dear! Can TV really be blamed for this, or me, for that matter? I didn't invent the magical-backdrop, magical-sense-screen. Certainly, it does have an effect! How could it not? AND they are 5-7-5-ers. See what I mean? Will the power of tv never cease to amaze? As an enabling device it has a lot to offer miscreants, deviants, they with the evil, receptive eye. *just a glimpse^*
                    of a tasteful backside
                        turns to what's behind If not yet convinced of the benefits of this great technological advance let me offer up to the God of outraged tradition another example. This one often returns while unseeing TV, moving slowly to an indeterminate yet tangible conclusion, like some night dreams I, who only daydream, am told about by those who do. Usually, it starts with a question followed by an image. More accurately, it is an inchoate, constantly juxtaposing or contrasting or oppositional **mass** of images, which culminates in a torrent of feely/touchy thought sensations that bubble and spread around, overlaying and making an illuminating coherence

incoherent. And if that seems irrational, watch this space! *name of the tree/means something to you/nothing to the tree* or does it? It may; it may not. Even at the most serene of serene moments, even at the deepest of our deepest deep, even experiencing exercises designed to aid maturation, however sensitively empathetic, no human really *knows* what it is like to be a tree, whether or not the tree likes to be named, likes the human-given name, or even has the slightest awareness of the concept of this urgent human requirement *to name?* Can it respond to what is projected onto it, and everything else for that matter? A tree, the one i can see in my garden, not the one flown into somebody's television programme, seems to react to light, dark, sun, rain, hot, cold, ageing, and much else, but what it is like to be a tree, its *quintessential nature,* belongs to it alone. Notice how I project an 'essence' into that blameless object! *Projection! There is little more to it than that.* All else is a mind blinding illusion. Of course, it must be something to be a tree, a bird, a whale, a racoon. What that is only a tree, bird, whale, racoon can know or not know, as the case may be.

another squirrel
praying into his last nuts
a bit longer^

All this from one evening spent using and misusing TV, our modernist bible medium of simplicity and addiction! Can more be asked of one piece of innovation? Indeed, (another rhetorical question rears its medusa head) where would avant-garde pursuits be without it? *a postscript conclusion   to metaphysics — in time for the football match*

cloud calligraphy
a hieroglyph
hard to decipher

hip hip hooray.   a small cheer for tv

* *dick petitt*

^ *dick petitt and stanley pelter*

diary letter

lingering days
pile up
the past recedes

Buson

Lying elsewhere. On the grass. Across its svelte green. Relaxed. Legs crossed. White capped cobblestone clouds. They dissemble into that mid blue of many summer skies. Slow moving. To somewhere over tree-speckled hilltops. Beyond the valley.

suns strobe
even within birdsong
the air is breathless

A tomboy girl, (coming on six) wears a ra ra skirt within a pink harmony of clothes. Kicks a full-size toy football. Hard. Way past her mother and sleeping sister (coming on one). On a heel she swishes a full circle, whistles and inexactly claps her hands. Mother. Blonde (dyed). Not long past her best tomboy years. Weighty. Runs her jostling breasts to collect the ball. Kicks it back. Hard. Such an effort. Angles of arms and legs crease the air. Pushes head back and lower. Nearly falls. For a while a wind is helpful.

your hair
combed by a soft wind
a gentle sweep back

Then i think of U. Eyes close. Then i see U. Keep them closed. Imagine what it would be like to be without you. Shudder. Not wanting to anymore, I open them. That's better.

Mona Lisa smile -
inside, an echo
of your voice

More than better. Quiver Happy.   i thought U would want to know.